Discovering
The National Trusts

John M. Parry

MACMILLAN

in association with
The National Trust

About this book

The National Trust was established in 1895. Its founders promised that any place of historic interest or natural beauty which came into their care could be looked after *for ever*. The main purpose of the Trust, and of the National Trust for Scotland which was formed in 1931, is to conserve such places for all time.

This book, a passport to the treasures of the two Trusts, will introduce you to homes of the past and show you how some of our ancestors lived; it will tell you about working places and the jobs people did in earlier times; and it will describe some of the many areas of extraordinary beauty owned by the Trusts and point out some of the problems of conserving them for the future.

There is practical information on the location of the properties and their main features, and a gazetteer section (Links Across the Country), arranged by area, which will tell you of related properties throughout the United Kingdom.

Children from the Alfriston Primary School in East Sussex pose outside the Clergy House, Alfriston (inset), which was near the point of collapse in 1893. It was the first building bought by the National Trust, in 1896 (for £10), and today it attracts over 20,000 visitors a year.

To Frances and Fiona and their generation

Text © John M. Parry 1983

Photographs (except those specified on page 128) © John M. Parry 1983

Designed by Robert Updegraff

First published 1983 by
MACMILLAN CHILDREN'S BOOKS
A division of Macmillan Publishers Limited
London and Basingstoke

Reprinted 1984

ISBN 0 333 35346 3 (book only)

ISBN 0 333 36719 7 (book and AA map)

British Library Cataloguing in Publication Data

Parry, John M.
Discovering the National Trusts
　　1. National Trust – Juvenile literature
　　2. National Trust for Scotland – Juvenile literature
　　3. Historic buildings – Great Britain – Juvenile literature
　　I. Title
　　914.1　　　DA660

Filmset in Apollo by Filmtype Services Limited, Scarborough, North Yorkshire.
Printed in Hong Kong

Contents

The Man who Collected Treasure

In 1980, during a *Blue Peter* television programme, some children buried a "Time Capsule", containing everyday things, in the foundations of a car park. Its purpose was to give anyone who discovered it hundreds of years from now an idea of life in Britain in 1980.

We only know about *our* past because of the things which have been left to us in *other* people's "Time Capsules" like castles, houses and private collections. Here is one.

A human magpie

Charles Wade began collecting in 1890 when he was seven years old. He bought knick-knacks, old buttons, bottles and tiny boxes and hated school where he said he learned very little. After fighting in World War I, he bought a large house with money his father had left him. He continued to buy and collect things all his life and began filling his house, Snowshill Manor, with treasure ranging from glass jars and swords to leather fire buckets and suits of armour.

He gave each of the sixteen large rooms odd names like Dragon, Zenith and Mermaid. Some he named after their colours like The Green Room or The Turquoise Hall. Other rooms give clues to their contents; for example, Admiral contains telescopes, compasses and swords. Everything in the house is exactly as it was when Mr Wade gave it to the National Trust in 1951. He died soon after but must have been pleased that he lived a life which followed his family motto so well – *Nequid Pereat!*

Below: *A Hundred Wheels. One of the rooms in Charles Wade's "Time Capsule" at Snowshill Manor.*

Let nothing perish!

Charles wrote that early childhood was the best part of anyone's life "before schools and schoolmasters have been able to destroy the greatest of all treasures – imagination!". As a result, his favourite room, called Seventh Heaven, is stacked with children's toys, including his own.

These are just some of the other 5,000 objects which are crammed into Charles Wade's "Time Capsule" at Snowshill: 27 smoking pipes; 224 drinking glasses; 22 walking sticks; 94 musical instruments; 34 model farm wagons; 52 dolls; 320 door keys; 38 clocks; 27 suits of Samurai armour; 26 spinning wheels; 22 children's prams and 18 wooden police truncheons!

There were so many things packed into the Manor House that there was not enough room for Charles Wade to live in it. Instead he chose to live in a small building next to the main house. This, too, is packed and crammed with all sorts of things in boxes, on shelves, dangling from the ceiling or tucked away in cupboards.

Below: *Seventh Heaven includes an 1850 train set, three dolls' houses, toy soldiers and model boats made by Mr Wade.*

Above: *Charles Wade's kitchen in the cottage is crammed with extraordinary things but there is no electricity.*

Below: *The Music Room has a Latin inscription over the door which means "Man is carried to heaven on the wings of music." At the top of the stairs another Latin motto reads: "For me today, for him tomorrow, after that who knows?"*

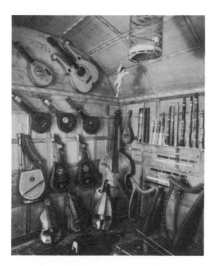

Treasure seeking

This is what Charles wrote about his collecting:

"Great has been the delight of forming my collection at Snowshill Manor – an enjoyment of many years for I started at the age of seven.
To how many interesting and out of the way places has it led me!
• to old cities, markets, sleepy country towns and peaceful, remote villages
• to ancient attics, chilly cellars and cobwebby crypts
• to houses rich and humble
• to old tumble-down sheds, patched and propped, with dim, mysterious interiors, heaped high with the mouldering accumulations of the Ages".

The treasure collected and stored at Snowshill Manor about 60 years ago is easy to explore. It is not so easy if the "Time Capsule" is over 1,000 years old and 5 metres under ground.

Buried Treasure

For years people had talked of Roman ruins buried in Chedworth Wood but it was only the interest of a labourer and a gamekeeper which led to their dramatic discovery in 1863.

The rabbits' secret

William Plumb was fascinated by old things and when he heard rumours of Roman treasure in Chedworth Wood, he decided to investigate. As he entered the Wood, his interest increased when he noticed several large, grey snails which he knew were the same type that the Romans had brought with them to Britain. There was a gamekeeper's cottage nearby and he asked for permission to investigate further. The gamekeeper agreed enthusiastically and took William a little way up a track where he showed him a number of rabbit burrows.

Outside each hole there were piles of small, square, coloured stones and pieces of broken pottery which had been thrown up by the rabbits.

"Now what d'you make of that?" said the gamekeeper. The two men started digging with their hands and half a metre down they found a large earthen pan with fingermarks on the side – made when the clay was still soft.

Encouraged by this excellent start, they moved further along the track to yet more burrows. This time there was rich, black soil at the entrances which suggested wood ash to the two men, and in the dark soil they found oyster shells and bones of small animals.

"Could this be a Roman rubbish tip?" thought William.

They searched more burrows and after digging around one of them, they uncovered a piece of mosaic flooring.

This was proof that they were on to something big, but it was getting dark and William had to return home. He was determined to explore the site another day but he feared that this might not be for a while because he "had to toil for his bread" and it was difficult to get time off work.

Below: *Rooms along the north wing of Chedworth. This was where William and Thomas first began their diggings in the Wood.*

The "gate post" stones which were found later are propped up against the wall.

Below left: *The mosaic dining room floor found by Giles and Billy Coates (see "Finding zummat") still has to be protected from people poking it.*

Above and below: *Excavations allow archaeologists to piece together what life must have been like at Chedworth 1,700 years ago. The baths were heated by an underfloor hot air system called a hypocaust. Baths were treated more like pubs as places to chat and meet socially. Artists' impressions based on firm archaeological evidence bring visits to the site alive.*

"Finding zummat"

Sadly there are no further records of William Plumb but we know that the gamekeeper, Thomas Margetts, wrote to Lord Eldon, the owner of Chedworth, about his discoveries and that proper excavations of the site began in 1864. The story is continued by Fred Norman – a local boy of fifteen:

"We began digging on a Monday morning and the first thing we came to was a stone stood upright like a gatepost. Close by was another stone and we found, I should think, about half a dozen all stood up. We found out after that was what a floor was laid on. Oh, we thought it was wonderful seeing these stones and we thought we were finding zummat. Then about three o'clock Giles and Billy Coates went and sunk a round hole and they came upon a pavement and fetched the rest of us."

The next morning 50 men dug out the rest of the room and revealed a mosaic floor. People came with their umbrellas and sticks to poke the floor and they had to be stopped.

On 28 June 1864, it was reported that 3,000 visitors came to the Roman villa – for this is what Thomas Margetts and William Plumb had uncovered. It was a fine example of a house occupied by Britons under Roman rule between AD 180 and 350, and is visited today by over 60,000 people every year.

Towers of Strength

Castles have tended to last longer than houses because they were built more for compact strength than spacious comfort. The castles of the 13th century were usually single stone towers. They were difficult to attack and many of them have lasted to this day.

The tower at Drum

You might think that a tower is a simple building, but take a look at the 25-metre high tower of Drum in Scotland. In the days before guns, height was important so that the defenders were well out of reach of their attackers on to whom they threw large stones or boiling liquids.

The walls slope outwards from a thickness of 0.9 metres at the top to 3.6 metres at the bottom. This gave the tower its strength and meant that an attacker could not hide directly up against the wall. The angle of the walls caused stones that were thrown from the top to bounce haphazardly off the bottom of the wall.

The tower corners are rounded to prevent the corner stones being rammed out of place, and the only entrance is a door a third of the way up the wall. When it was built in the 1280s, there were wooden steps up to it which were removed in times of attack. The high battlements and the few, small windows complete this truly defensive tower of strength.

Above: *Drum Castle from the south east. The original 13th-century defensive tower is on the right – the rest was added over 300 years later.*

Inside the door to the tower there is a strong frame of iron squares called a "yett". This gave added protection from attack. See Crathes (right).

"Wha dare meddle wi' me?"

At first glance Craigievar Castle (*right*) looks the perfect defensive house built on top of a high tower. Thick walls slope outwards towards the bottom; the corners are rounded; and the windows are small. But look at its position. The ground which rises to the left gives attackers a height advantage. The door is on the ground floor, not a third of the way up the wall, and the stone balustrade at the top of the castle is hardly a strong battlement like the one at Drum.

A closer look at another Scots tower house called Crathes (*below*) shows some more cracks in the defence. The walls are covered in small stones, called harling, which gives a smarter appearance but which would disintegrate quickly under attack.

There are no battlements. Instead there is only a design at the top of the tower. Even the cannons underneath the turrets are not real but are stone copies.

Crathes and Craigievar were built to *look* strong by borrowing some of the old ideas of defence. Their purpose was to show the power of their owners whose motto was, "Wha dare meddle wi' me?" Their message is one of defiance rather than defence. Luckily for us the local people did not challenge their masters and so these extraordinary houses stand today.

Above: *Craigievar, a fairy-tale home built from 1600 to 1626.*

Below: *Crathes. Built to impress but not for real defence. Look at the position of the iron "yett" on the outside of a ground floor door.*

A move outwards

By the middle of the 16th century, height was not so necessary for defence because of the invention of firearms. Protective L-shaped walls from which a shot could be fired were much more useful and so castles were extended outwards with lower and longer walls.

Drum Castle, unlike Crathes and Craigievar, was built near an important crossroads and continued to be a defensive site until the 17th century. In 1513 the owners built a lower extension round the tower which gave them more room and better defence against pistols.

As time passed, defence became less important and so Drum was extended even further.

In 1619, a whole new house was added to the tower and its L-shaped extensions. This house included a small rounded turret with a roof like a cone which was built for decoration rather than defence.

In 1845, the first floor of the original 13th-century tower was converted into a library and a large window with a rounded top was put into the east wall.

In the 1880s, a large hall and front door were added to the north front as well as a wide corridor which ran the full length of the house. Finally, a modern arch and courtyard, added this century, completes the shape of Drum.

The home that we see today is a mixture of defence and safe comfort which dates from 1280 until 1885. It is a castle which grew into a home, unlike Crathes and Craigievar which were homes that were built to look like castles.

The Castle with the Soft Centre

True defensive sites are often so dramatic and attractive that people are tempted to convert them into homes. This is the story of one castle which was turned into a home by a brilliant young architect called Edwin Lutyens.

Beat the tide

Lindisfarne Castle lies at the southern end of a strip of land which is cut off twice daily from the Northumberland coast by the sea.

The tide comes in so quickly that it has claimed many lives and in the past reckless people who wandered from the staked track risked their lives in the treacherous quicksands. Today there is a tarmac road across the sands but still people are caught if they cross too late and their only hope is to abandon their car, wade through the rising water to a white rescue box and sit out the tide for six hours.

The Castle was built in 1548 to defend a small harbour which had become a useful haven for boats guarding the north-east coast. By 1820, it was no longer needed as a fort and for a while it became a coastguard station before it eventually stood bleak and empty.

In 1900, Edward Hudson, who owned the magazine *Country Life*, visited the island and scrambled over the walls of the old castle. Although it had been abandoned, the strong walls were in a good condition and he decided to buy it. A castle cut off from the mainland twice a day, perched on top of a 30-metre crag overlooking a harbour, and exposed to mighty North Sea gales was too tempting a site to resist.

" . . . Have got Lindisfarne stop"

This short telegram brought Edwin Lutyens, then 33 years old, to Lindisfarne. His job was to convert the cold, deserted, bare, stone castle into a friendly, snug, comfortable home.

Below: *The Lindisfarne causeway is flooded twice a day and the tide still catches people today.* Left: *Several years ago a petrol lorry and driver were stranded for six hours out of reach of the white rescue box on stilts on the bridge.* Right: *The view from the rescue box at low tide. The sea covers the whole line of posts at high tide.*

Above: *The Castle and its dramatic position inspired Edwin Lutyens, who made clever use of the rounded ceilings and walls. He designed the round table for the dining room* (top left) *and his arches, round pillars and curved steps* (top right) *help soften the cold passages. So do the herringbone floor patterns* (bottom left). *In the sitting room* (bottom right) *there are steps in the thick walls and rounded curtains that cover the walls in the daytime.*

Lutyens achieved his cosy effect by putting as much as possible of the L-shaped castle and its old rooms to very different uses. The ammunition store and cellar became a dining room and sitting room. He turned the lower battery into a large hall and kitchen, and he joined a separate guard house to the castle by a long gallery, or hallway.

The stairs and passages still have their original, rough stone walls, but Lutyens used smoother stones in the main rooms and took advantage of the thick walls by building little steps up to the window ledges which he made wide enough to sit on. He designed special curtains which cover the inside walls when they are not drawn across the windows.

Red bricks laid in a herring-bone pattern help to soften the look of the floors, and the low ceilings, wide but short windows and rounded arches throughout the castle all combine to make it a warm and cosy home inside.

In 1944, Lindisfarne was given to the Trust, whose job it has been to conserve this very special castle and to keep it looking the same as it did when it was used as a family home.

11

Read the Walls

The outside walls of old houses often hold a surprising amount of information about their history. Up to the 17th century, only important buildings like castles and churches were built with expensive stone. Most houses were made of oak because large forests grew over much of Britain, and timber was easy and cheap to cut. It could also be carved to make attractive decorations; it was strong but flexible and houses built with timber frames were popular. Their walls were made of wattle and daub which was a mixture of clay, cow dung, straw and animal hair held together by woven sticks and finished with a coat of plaster.

During the 17th century, with the supply of oak starting to run out, builders began to use different local materials. They used flint in South and East England, limestone in the Cotswolds, slate in Wales and granite in Cornwall. In the clay regions, and especially in East Anglia, bricks were made by baking the clay in kilns.

As transport improved in the 18th century, building materials could be carried more easily around the country. Bricks, in particular, became the most popular material because, unlike stone, they did not have to be cut or shaped in any way – they were all the same "standard" size.

In the 19th century, as industries and cities grew and developed, the lives and needs of people changed. Rows of terraced houses sprang up and tall tenement buildings for workers were designed so that more people could live in less space.

In our century many older buildings have disappeared to make room for new factories, warehouses and shopping precincts. Offices and tower blocks made of glass and concrete have been "purpose-built" to suit the needs of city dwellers. Little decoration is added to these concrete and glass buildings and there is a danger that eventually our cities could look much the same. Petrol stations and supermarkets may be more convenient, but there is little to catch your eye except the "latest offers". It is important to preserve fine examples of old buildings with different materials, styles and decorations – we may even want to copy some of them one day.

Top: *Lyveden New Bield. It was never lived in.*

Middle: *Bernard Ward and his wife Lady Anne disagreed about most things. In the 1760s, they built a house called Castle Ward in Northern Ireland. Bernard wanted a straight "classical" style of house. His wife wanted a church-like Gothic style. So they compromised. One half of the house is Classical, the other Gothic!*

Bottom left: *Thomas Windham built Felbrigg Hall in the 1620s. The builder showed off his skills by emphasising the details. The chimneys loom; the windows are large; there is a grand, carved entrance. The builder is saying, "Look what I can do", and the owner is saying, "Look what I can afford to do!"*

Fifty years later, Windham's son added a Classical wing to Felbrigg (above). There is no porch; the chimneys are low; everything is in proportion. The standard-sized bricks brought order and mathematical symmetry.

Bottom right: *Little Moreton Hall. A timber-framed 16th-century house bursting with detail!*

The walls of Lyveden New Bield

The walls of this house with no roof (*top right*) tell the story of the Passion and Death of Christ. The house was begun in 1594 by Sir Thomas Tresham who was an ardent but persecuted Catholic. He designed the house as a Cross and included religious stone carvings all round it (*left*).

In 1600, Sir Thomas was imprisoned for his religious beliefs and died in 1605. A few months later, his eldest son was involved in the Gunpowder Plot and died a prisoner in the Tower of London. The house was never completed.

In the Civil War of 1642–51 Cromwell's troops stripped the house of its valuable timber. Today its walls stand alone, dignified and serene with a story to tell.

Save Erddig!

The outsides of buildings may provide a record of styles and techniques using different materials but the insides of buildings contain a store of information about the way people used to live.

Sometimes a particular house may contain so much "inside information" that it is worth rescuing at all costs — even if the house is showing serious signs of disintegration. Such was the case with Erddig.

Lives in verse

The house stands on top of a coalfield near Wrexham in North Wales and contains a superb collection of 18th-century furniture. But Erddig differs from many country houses because it also contains a rich amount of information about life "below stairs" — in the kitchens, the carpenters' shop, laundry, bakehouse, garden and the blacksmiths' forge.

The Yorke family, who owned Erddig, were so interested in the people who worked for them that they painted and photographed their servants and wrote rhyming verses about them. In 1852, Sarah Davies was a dairy maid:

> ... in everything she well did please,
> Save in the art of making cheese.

Thomas Murray was a butler at the time:

> ... clever was he at drawing cork,
> And a good hand at knife and fork.

In 1911, the head gardener was George Roberts:

> ... our children greet him as their friend
> Pleased when to him their help they lend,
> And honoured feel when asked to take
> A turn at barrow, spade or rake.

Above and below: *The State Bedroom before and after restoration. The bed was in another room because of the dangerous state of the ceiling.*

Left: *Some of the portraits of and poems about the servants who worked at Erddig hang on the walls of the servants' hall. This record of life below stairs made Erddig a most unusual and interesting country house that had* to *be saved.*

Rescue

Above and below: *The carpenters' workshop before and after restoration. Now it is used for repairs and carpentry on the estate and for making benches and tables for outside use at other Trust places.*

Times change and by 1966 things had gone badly wrong. Simon Yorke, who had been living alone at Erddig with two part-time servants for over 40 years, died without making a will. His younger brother Philip moved in and soon had to cope with big problems. Mining subsidence had caused the house to sink 1½ metres at one end and 1 metre at the other. Rainwater poured through gaps in the roof. The walls bulged; ceilings groaned; wallpaper hung in tattered strips; the garden was a jungle. The house was literally falling apart, and yet it contained one of the finest collections of furniture in the country and a unique record of the servants who had worked there.

Philip rigged up crude anti-burglar devices to protect the priceless treasures in their mouldering surroundings. He stacked a pile of empty dog food tins on a table in the basement and attached it to a door knob with a piece of string. He put battery-powered pressure pads under the Hall carpet which rang a bell if they were stepped on. He even kept a .22 rifle at his bedside (although the firing pin was missing)!

Instead of selling his treasures for a fortune, he finally gave Erddig and its contents to the National Trust in 1973, after a seven-year struggle to keep the house in one piece.

Long, Dark Evenings

The Browne family lived in Townend from 1623 to 1943. They were farmers in the Lake District and their farmhouse is filled with their everyday possessions which were used in the house for over 300 years.

They carved and made most of their furniture, and every part of the house gives a clue to what life must have been like during the hard days and the long nights of the 17th, 18th and 19th centuries.

Strike a light

Before electricity, light was provided by burning candles and rush lights. The candles were made out of animal fat and the popular home-produced rush lights were made from rushes or "sieves". These were picked in late summer and cut into lengths of about 35 cms. Most of the outer rind was peeled off except for one thin strip which was left in order to give the "sieve" some strength. After it had been dipped in bacon fat and left to dry, it was ready to light. The secret was to keep it at an angle of about 45 degrees so that it burnt slowly and steadily. The smell of the spluttering rushes must have been strong and not very pleasant.

Tinder boxes were used to make fire. They contained a metal striker and a piece of flint which was hit to produce a spark which ignited a piece of rag or straw. It could be a slow and frustrating job but it was necessary in the days before matches.

Above: *One corner of the kitchen at Townend has a "fitted" clock and cupboards. From right to left on the dresser are a rushlight in a holder; a tinder box; a portable candle and sieve holder; and a glass bowl* (see opposite).
Below: *Tinder box. A spark was produced by striking a flint on metal. You hoped this would ignite the dry tinder in the tin!*

My poor daughter Agnes

The Brownes built themselves "fitted" cupboards and drawers which they used as a filing system for everything from receipts, bills and shopping lists to details of sheep or scraps of paper with scribbled names and addresses on them.

Three hundred years of family documents are crammed into 18 books and ledgers which lie waiting to be investigated and which can tell us so much about the Brownes' past. Even one little sheet of paper carries a lot of information. Look at the expenses (*below*) for the burial of Benjamin Browne's poor little four-year-old daughter, Agnes, who died of smallpox in 1694:

- a great many people were expected as 40 lb of cheese is a lot and there was a lot of bread too. Funerals were not just family occasions but concerned the whole community
- there were many people who were "officially" poor
- the high charge for a sermon suggests the importance of God's blessing on Agnes and indeed the whole community
- look at the value of a veal skin
- the farmers were out making hay while the sun shone. It was so desperately important to get grain in for the long hard winter that even a free feast had to be turned down
- there are no costs for anything to drink which indicates that alcohol was brewed by the family at home
- "our Peggy" probably refers to a servant
- Agnes' grandfather gave some money towards the expenses to help out a little.

The costs raise some questions too. Was the tobacco really for smoking or was it used on Agnes' body in some way? Was the very small piece of worsted just a band of cloth or a ribbon, and why was the cost of breaking a grave inside the Church much more than digging it?

Above: *The Brownes increased their candle power by filling a glass bowl with water. This refracted the light to produce a brighter beam.*

Right: *The burial costs of Agnes Browne are given in pounds, shillings and pence. There were 12 pence to one shilling and 20 shillings to one pound.*

A pound weight is approx. 450 grams and 2 yards (yds) is about 1.8 metres.

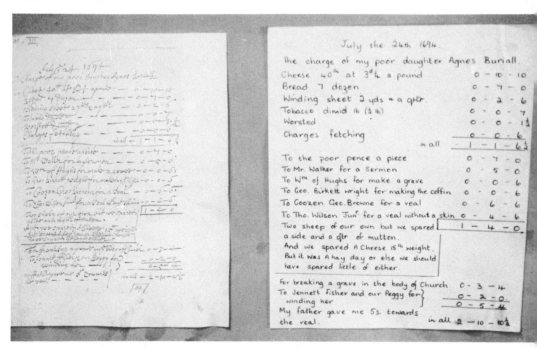

Switch on Cragside

In the past, before the discovery of modern medicines, many children died young or became ill quickly and often.

The Kingfisher of Rothbury

William Armstrong was a weak child who coughed his way through each winter. He had to spend his winters indoors at home in Newcastle but he was seldom bored because he invented toy machines for himself which he powered by dropping weights over the stair banister.

Every summer, his parents took him on holiday to the countryside around Rothbury, about 20 miles (32 km) north of Newcastle, where the fresh air was good for William's lungs. He spent his precious summers fishing and exploring the pools of the Debden stream which ran along the bottom of a steep valley dominated by a rocky crag. He spent so much time fishing that his family nicknamed him "the Kingfisher".

By the age of 26, he had become a solicitor, but still enjoyed tinkering with machines, inventing and fishing. One day he had an idea:

> "I was lounging idly about, watching an old watermill, when it occurred to me what a small part of the power of the water was used in driving the wheel and then I thought how great would be the force of even a small quantity of water if its energy were only concentrated in one column."

He began inventing engines and machines powered by water and finally left his job as a lawyer to become an engineer and manufacturer. He built Newcastle's water supply system, invented a water-powered crane and went on to manufacture rifles, guns and armaments which eventually led to the formation of the Vickers Armstrong company.

Above: *Debden stream, haunt of the "Kingfisher", and in the distance his house – Cragside.*

Left: *Part of the 6-mile (10-km) system of water pipes and wooden troughs built to bring water from the moor to the generating station. In 1883, Armstrong said that whenever the time came for using the power of great waterfalls, the transmission of power by electricity would become a system of vast importance. In 1895, the Canadian Niagara Falls were harnessed to generate electricity and the project manager, Dr Muirhead, visited Cragside twice saying that this gave him the idea for Niagara.*

Water on the brain

Memories of his happy childhood flooded back in 1863 when he revisited Rothbury for the first time in 30 years. He decided to build a house overlooking the stream and called it Cragside. He eventually bought 1,725 acres on which he planted *7 million* trees and built four lakes to supply the house with drinking and washing water. Water also provided power to work a lift. Water operated the central heating system and water turned a roasting spit in the kitchen. But in 1878 water provided power for something far more important . . .

Above: *The Library where Joseph Swan's electric bulbs were used in the first kerosene lamps in the world to be converted to electricity. When the whole system was properly wired, Armstrong invited the 13-year-old pantry boy, Andrew Crozier, to switch on Cragside.*

Electric light

Below: *The converted kerosene lamps were lit by placing the enamelled copper vase on a base which contained an insulated cup of mercury. A bare wire, dipped in the mercury, carried the electricity to the bulb and the return current was conducted down the copper sides of the vase. The lamp was turned off by simply lifting the vase from its base!*

The first electric light at Cragside was an arc lamp which produced a yellow light that buzzed noisily. Before it could be used, the butler had to send a message (by swinging a paraffin lamp) to a man in the generating shed who then opened the sluice gates which let in water to start the electric turbine running. The power was carried along a cable laid in a wooden trough on trestles above the ground.

Two year later, in 1880, his friend, the inventor Joseph Swan, demonstrated a new "light bulb" which burned in a vacuum rather than in the open air like the arc light. Armstrong was so impressed that he asked Swan to try out his new bulbs at Cragside. With great excitement they set up the lamps and turned on the power. At first the current was too strong and the bulbs burned too brightly but Armstrong was in no doubt that they were seeing the light of the future.

It was steady, noiseless and clear and within two months, Swan had installed 45 lamps around the house. They could be turned on or off by small switches attached to the wall – a slight turn and the lamps immediately lit up. It was like magic!

Forty-four years after his first thoughts about water power, the Kingfisher had landed his finest catch – Cragside, the first house *in the world* to be lit by hydro-electric power.

19

Escape from Moseley

When the Queen abandoned her Range Rover for the safety of an hotel during a blizzard in 1981, it made headline news and a plaque in the bar commemorates the rare event.

No such plaque exists at Moseley Old Hall but 330 years earlier another monarch, King Charles II, had also taken refuge – not from a blizzard but from soldiers after his head.

Deadly hide and seek

In 1651, a Civil War raged in England between Government troops led by Cromwell and Royalist forces led by their 21-year-old King, Charles II. On 3 September, the King was defeated at Worcester and, after fleeing northwards, he made his way, via the Boscobel oak, to the house of Thomas Whitgreave.

Disguised as a woodcutter, the King and six bodyguards arrived in the dead of night on 8 September. They were met at the back door by Whitgreave and Father John Huddlestone, a Catholic priest, who was giving private lessons to Whitgreave's two young nephews and a friend who were all staying at Moseley.

Charles was led upstairs and introduced to his hosts who had not recognised their King in disguise. They fell to their knees and after thanking them for their help, Charles asked, "Where is the private place my Lord tells me of?"

Above: *Plaque at The Crossed Hands, Old Sodbury, Avon.*

"The best place I was ever in"

The hiding place was a small room built between two bedrooms. The entrance to it was through a false panel in one of the bedroom walls which had a trick catch to open it. The secret room had two removable floorboards and underneath them was a small hole with a bed of straw and an exit to a chimney. It was perfect and well used as a refuge by Father Huddlestone because the Catholic church was banned in England and priests went in fear of their lives.

The king took one look at the room and smiled. "It's the best place I was ever in."

Lookout duty

Charles changed out of his soggy clothes, Father Huddlestone bathed the King's aching feet and Whitgreave brought him "biskett" and a glass of wine. They talked excitedly until dawn when the exhausted King collapsed and slept in a bed for the first time since the battle.

In the morning, the servants were sent away on various errands, but the cook was asked to stay to prepare meals "for a soldier in the house". The three young boys were told the same story and were given time off lessons to keep a lookout from an attic window for approaching soldiers.

The day passed quietly and at supper the youngest boy, John Palin, made everyone laugh when he shouted, "Eat hard boys! For we have been on the life guard and hard duty this day." Lookout duty was much more fun for John than boring old lessons, but little did he realise that the King of England was in his care. Another night passed safely, but the next afternoon the cook rushed upstairs shouting, "Soldiers, soldiers are coming!" Charles was bundled into the hole. Whitgreave carefully closed the floorboards over his head, clicked the door shut, eased the panel back into the wall, took a deep breath and walked calmly downstairs to face the soldiers.

The rest "is history", as people say. The trick worked. Charles eventually escaped to France and returned to London $8\frac{1}{2}$ years later. We know the *precise* details of his escape because people wanted to hear his dramatic story which could only be told when he was restored to the Throne in 1660. Today the house stands by a busy motorway. It holds the story of just three nights and two days — only a slice of history. Nothing grand, rich or pompous — just a moment to hold your breath and wonder.

Below: *A schoolboy from the local Thomas Whitgreave School crouches in the royal hiding place.*

A Restless Mind

While Charles II was running for his life during the Civil War in 1651, a nine-year-old boy living quietly at Woolsthorpe Manor in Lincolnshire was beginning to show that he had a brain which would make him as famous as the young King.

A sober, silent thinking lad

Isaac Newton did not have much of a start to life. His father, a farmer, died three months before Isaac's birth on Christmas Day, 1642. He was a small, weak baby who was lucky to survive his first few days. His mother re-married when he was three, but his step-father would not allow the young boy in his house, so Isaac lived alone with his grandmother at Woolsthorpe.

Playing alone made him inventive. When he was nine, he made his own accurate sundial to tell the time and measured the strength of storms by comparing jumps he made on windy days with measurements of jumps he had made on calm days. He asked awkward questions like, "How can flies walk on water without wetting their feet?". He was absent-minded too. Once he led a horse up a steep hill but forgot to remount at the top and walked the rest of the long journey home leading the horse behind him while he daydreamed in a world of his own.

Surrounded by death

Despite Isaac's absent-mindedness, he passed into Cambridge University in 1661 where he studied sciences and became so involved in his work that he frequently forgot to eat meals. He stuffed

Below: *Newton used a piece of specially shaped glass called a prism for his experiments on light. His notes recording the angle of the sun, the size and shape of the coloured image on the wall, and the distance of 22 feet* exactly *from the prism to the wall, suggest that his crucial experiment was conducted at Woolsthorpe Manor in August 1665.*

Above: *The south-facing window which Newton used for his experiments on light.*

Right: *Woolsthorpe Manor — the pot of gold at the end of the "spectrum".*

scribbled solutions to mathematical problems in his desk and was always ready to tackle puzzles which had baffled other scholars for years.

But, in the summer of 1666, disaster struck. The Great Plague, a deadly and highly infectious disease, spread north from London and 7,000 bodies a week were being hurled into mass graves. Cambridge was evacuated and its students fled to the countryside. Isaac Newton returned to his childhood home where, during the next two quiet years, he made great discoveries about gravity and light. In the orchard a falling apple sparked off a train of thought that eventually led him to realise that the fall of the apple and the movement of the moon were due to the *same force*. In his darkened study he carried out experiments which showed that sunlight was not white but a mixture of colours which he called the spectrum. These discoveries have been called some of the greatest achievements ever made in science.

Newton himself put it more humbly in a letter to a friend just before his death in 1727 at the grand age of 85. He wrote:

"I do not know what I may appear to the World but to myself I seem to have been only like a little boy playing on the seashore, and diverting myself by now and then finding a smoother pebble or a prettier shell than ordinary, while the great ocean of truth lay all undiscovered before me."

Word Capsules

Poets capture thoughts, feelings or events by using language in a powerful and memorable way. Many poems are difficult to understand, but some of William Wordsworth's poetry and descriptions are easier to follow. He described Sir Isaac Newton as ''a mind forever voyaging through strange seas of Thought, alone''. As for the colours of the spectrum, he wrote:

> *My heart leaps up when I behold*
> *A rainbow in the sky:*
> *So was it when my life began;*
> *So is it now I am a man;*
> *So be it when I shall grow old,*
> *Or let me die!*

Above: *Part of the Lake District which inspired Wordsworth so much. This is Ullswater, near the woods of Gowbarrow Park where Dorothy and William walked on 15 April 1802.*

Wordsworth lived in the Lake District and many of his poems are about Nature and the countryside, from the big and grand:

> *High on a mountain's highest ridge,*
> *Where oft the stormy winter gale*
> *Cuts like a scythe, while through the clouds*
> *It sweeps from vale to vale.*

to the small and humble:

> *I've watched you now a full half-hour*
> *Self-poised upon that yellow flower;*
> *And little butterfly! indeed*
> *I know not if you sleep or feed.*

Childhood

William Wordsworth was born at Cockermouth in April 1770 where he spent eight happy years in a house with a large garden which backed on to a river. He had three brothers and a little sister, Dorothy, whom he adored. They played hide and seek, chased butterflies and hunted for birds' nests along a terrace at the end of the garden.

Beyond the terrace was a river which William called "a Playmate whom we dearly lov'd". Their summers shone:

> Oh! many a time have I, a five years Child,
> A naked Boy, in one delightful Rill,
> A little Mill-race sever'd from his stream,
> Made one long bathing of a summer's day,
> Bask'd in the sun, and plunged, and bask'd again.

Below: *The terrace walk at the end of the garden where William and Dorothy played as children.*

William was a naughty boy with a quick temper and rapidly changing moods which his mother found difficult. "He will be remarkable either for good or evil," she told a friend shortly before her death in 1778. William was eight.

His heartbroken father died five years later. The happy days were over and Dorothy went to live with relations in Halifax while William stayed with an uncle in Penrith. Brother and sister were not to meet for nine long years and when they revisited their home many years later, Dorothy wrote:

All was ruin! the terrace walk buried and choked up with the old privet hedge ... the same hedge where the sparrows were used to build their nests!

The house continued to rot but was saved from demolition in 1937 when local people launched a campaign that attracted Wordsworth lovers from all over the English-speaking world. In 1939 they were able to buy the house and with it the memories of a famous childhood in a garden we can still visit.

I wandered lonely . . .

William and Dorothy never forgot their happy days at Cockermouth and remained fond of each other all their lives. She helped William with his poetry and kept a detailed diary of their times together. Here is part of her account for Thursday 15 April 1802, which led to Wordsworth's most famous poem:

Below: *Wordsworth's birthplace at Cockermouth, Cumbria.*

... when we were in the woods beyond Gowbarrow Park we saw a few daffodils close to the water side. We fancied that the lake had floated the seeds ashore and that the little colony had so sprung up. But as we went along there were more and yet more and at last under the boughs of the trees, we saw that there was a long belt of them along the shore, about the breadth of a country turnpike road. I never saw daffodils so beautiful ... some rested their heads upon these stones as on a pillow for weariness and the rest tossed and reeled and danced ...

Two years later William wrote about a host of golden flowers which have become locked in his most famous word capsule — a poem we simply call "Daffodils".

Every Picture Tells a Story

An old man at breakfast once spilt some cream by mistake over a young lady's new dress during a visit to friends in the country. He did not apologise but rushed upstairs and, just before lunch, brought down a painting of the incident which he gave the young lady. The artist who found it easier to apologise with a painting rather than words was Joseph Mallord William Turner. The house where he was staying was Petworth, which belonged to his friend and patron, the 3rd Earl of Egremont.

Different backgrounds

The two men had been brought up in very different circumstances. Turner was half the age of Lord Egremont and began his career above his father's barber shop in London. He earned his living by selling small paintings and drawings to a magazine. Lord Egremont lived in a magnificent country house, on an income of over £200,000 a year, which he had first received at the age of twelve when his father died in 1763. He had many servants – Turner did not. He was an aristocrat – Turner was not. But they had one thing in common. They were both rebels. Turner had become tired of the old style of painting and wanted to paint pictures which were more exciting and colourful. The ageing Earl found little pleasure in the grand and pompous life of some of his rich friends. Instead he used his great wealth to provide hospitality for creative people in the hope that it would encourage them to produce great works of art. Turner was a bold, imaginative artist who experimented with colours and shapes which few people liked.

One art critic described a picture of a storm as ''all soapsuds and whitewash'', and a portrait of a young girl called Jessica was nick-named ''The Mustard Pot'' because Turner had used a yellow background.

But Lord Egremont liked Turner's pictures and encouraged the young artist to stay at Petworth as often as he wished.

Above: *J.M.W. Turner. Born 1775, died 1851. He is buried in St Paul's Cathedral, London.*

Below: *Turner's painting of Lord Egremont and his dogs in Petworth Park.*

When one critic said that he never saw sunsets the way Turner painted them, Turner looked him straight in the eye and replied, ''No, but wouldn't you like to?''

27 ✳ FÊTE IN PETWORTH PARK 9ᵗʰ JUNE 1835. *WITHERINGTON.*

Above: *At this Fête, Lord Egremont provided joints of beef and plum puddings and loaves "piled like cannon balls" for 6,000 local people, rich and poor.*

Below: *The Turner Room, Petworth. The bottom left painting on the far wall is the same view of the Park as from the window. It has a cricket match in place of Lord Egremont and his dogs.*

A lasting friendship

Over the years a true friendship developed between the rich, generous peer and the poor, talented artist. Turner painted many pictures of Petworth House and Park, as well as two of Lord Egremont's business projects, the Brighton Chain Pier and the Chichester canal. In the Brighton picture he painted some old vegetables, including carrots, floating in the sea.

"Carrots don't float," laughed Lord Egremont.

"Oh yes they do," replied Turner and, to prove the point, a servant was summoned to fetch some carrots and a bucket of water. The carrots sank but Turner kept them in his painting insisting that old carrots *would* float in salty sea water!

Another picture shows Lord Egremont, followed by a line of dogs, striding across Petworth Park at sunset. He was fond of animals but was horrified to see himself in the picture and he asked Turner to paint him out of it. Instead, Turner painted another picture of the same scene with a cricket match in place of the Earl. The first picture hangs in the Tate Gallery in London; the second hangs by a window which looks out on to the same view.

When Turner died he left a remarkable collection of oil paintings and watercolours to the Nation and is thought by many to have been Britain's greatest artist.

At Petworth today thirteen paintings hang in the Turner Room. Each tells a story, and a few of his bold and exciting paintings are now valued at more than £1 million *each.*

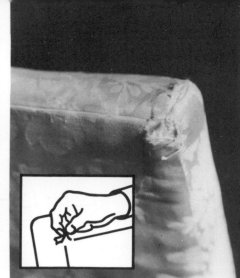

Please Don't Touch

Grand country houses have large, beautiful rooms. In the past, some of these rooms were used just once a year for a special occasion like a Royal visit. They were filled with expensive and impressive furniture, valuable paintings, precious carpets and lavish curtains.

The best way of protecting such important possessions was to use them rarely, and for most of the year the rooms remained locked and the furniture was protected by cotton "dust sheets".

Today, visitors want to see these rooms *because* of their wealth and beauty, but imagine the effect of 80,000 "guests" a year.

Problems

Some of the problems caused by thousands of visitors every year are obvious. Things get broken; carpets wear out; stiletto heels mark wooden floors; shoes with tracked soles bring in mud; and staircases become weakened by the extra weight they have to carry. But other problems are less obvious.

Country houses contain many objects which are made from natural materials. For example, the wood used in furniture once stood as trunks of living trees. The wool in tapestries and carpets was once on the backs of sheep. The silk in many textiles once formed the cocoons of the silk moth chrysalis; and the leather in book bindings and covers was once the skin of cows. Even the old, colourful dyes came originally from plants and insects. All these natural materials are composed of complicated organic compounds which eventually break down into simple compounds such as carbon dioxide gas and water. When this happens, dyes fade, textiles crumble into dust and leather rots.

This process of decay may be quite slow, but if we are not careful it can sometimes be very quick. Ultraviolet radiation from the sun speeds up the rate of decay. So do the sulphur fumes produced by burning oil and coal. Eventually the fumes turn to acid which attacks even the stones of our buildings and quickly destroys textiles, paper and leather. We also have to be careful not to allow houses to become too damp. Micro-organisms such as fungi and bacteria grow quickly in damp conditions and will actually "eat" organic materials such as cotton and wool.

Top left: *Beautiful seats once used by a single family cannot survive thousands of visitors "resting their legs" even for a minute or two.*

Above: *Some people even pick at the stitching on pieces of furniture.*

Above: *Humidity readings are taken outside and inside some of the rooms at Cotehele, Cornwall, as part of an experiment to try to assess, and repair, the damage from dampness.*

Solutions

The best solution is to shut the rooms all year except on special occasions – as they did in the past. That's why we've got the treasures of the past today. The next best solution is to turn the house into a museum of glass cases in darkened rooms, but this loses the atmosphere of a lived-in home. The balance between conservation and the enjoyment of old houses is a difficult one.

Some houses provide soft slippers to save wear and tear on the carpets and floors. Many rooms have blinds drawn against fierce sunlight. Others have had their windows sprayed with an expensive liquid which absorbs ultraviolet rays. On busy Bank Holidays the numbers of people entering a house may be controlled. But there are no easy solutions.

The special rooms which were so carefully protected in the past have been exposed to more light, dust and pollution in the last 15 years than in the previous 300 years. The five most important enemies of a country house and its treasures are sulphur dioxide, sunlight, dust, touching fingers and people who don't understand that conservation is about slowing down the process of decay so that people in the future will enjoy what we take for granted today.

Right: *Visitors do not always understand that some rooms need low levels of light in order to reduce the damage done by sunlight.*

Below: *Scratches and fingerprints are all part of the problems of conservation too.*

29

Hunt the Ceiling

History can be found in many different places – from paintings, poems and single rooms to whole houses, documents and castles. At archaeological sites, like Chedworth Roman Villa, we dig it up. In decaying houses, like Erddig, we can make better sense of it by restoring old things.

But occasionally history just pops up out of the blue.

The box

Knightshayes Court was gratefully received by the National Trust as a gift from Sir John Heathcoat-Amory in 1973.

Although the Victorian house was unusual, the Trust was more interested in the spectacular garden which Sir John and Lady Amory had designed and planted. It was, and still is, a rare and exciting garden.

In 1980, the Trust and Lady Amory decided that the time had come to make some changes to the house. Lady Amory was keen to re-decorate the Drawing Room so that some family pictures could be hung on the walls, and the Trust wanted to rewrite the guide book. They asked Hugh Meller, an art historian, to prepare the text.

Hugh wanted extra material to write about and so he rummaged through old papers and documents. In his searches he came across an old box which had not been opened for at least 40 years. He opened it gingerly and looked inside.

Above: *The Drawing Room ceiling at Knightshayes Court in 1979.*

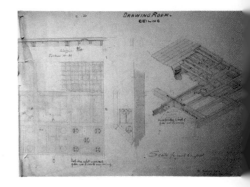

30

The box contained drawings of Knightshayes Court as it looked about 100 years ago. One particular sketch caught Hugh Meller's eye. It showed part of a blue and gold ceiling in the Drawing Room. Plans for such a ceiling had been drawn in 1873 by a famous architect called William Burges, but no-one thought that the ceiling had ever been started, let alone completed. Hugh wondered. In his hands was a sketch of the painted ceiling. Could it be that there was still a blue and gold painted ceiling above the present white one?

A day in November

The Trust cautiously agreed to investigate the Drawing Room ceiling, and in November 1980 a small hole was cut in the white plaster. Behind it was blue painted wood in perfect condition. To the left another hole revealed a brown strip of wood with a red painted line. To the right, another hole sparkled with a glint of gold paint.

Over the next two months, workmen took down fifteen white plaster panels to reveal the whole beautiful ceiling with its gold "jellymould" designs. The Victorian house had suddenly become as interesting as the garden.

When the last panel was removed, a piece of paper fluttered to the floor. On it were the names of five workmen who had been ordered to cover up the ceiling on 12 September 1889. *They* knew that they were covering up something beautiful and important. The little scrap of paper was their personal record of a moment of history for someone else to discover 91 years later. They knew that *one* day their scribbles would fall, like the ceiling, as "gold out of the blue".

Above: *Work in progress during November 1980.*

Below: *The ceiling today.*

The Homes in Part One

Where to find them

Directions are given to the nearest kilometre and mile, and include, where relevant, map references based on the 1:50 000 Series of Ordnance Survey maps. After each main entry there is a list of associated places from all over the United Kingdom. Extra details and directions for these are given on the page numbers shown in brackets.

1 *The Man Who Collected Treasure* (page 4)

Snowshill Manor is in *Gloucestershire*, 5 km (3 miles) S of the W end of Broadway, 6 km (4 miles) W of the junction of A44 and A424.

Other homes with unusual collections include Tatton Park, *Cheshire* (112); Erddig, *Clwyd* (107); Trerice, *Cornwall* (98); Sudbury Hall, *Derbyshire* (112); Arlington Court, Buckland Abbey, Overbecks, *Devon* (98); Dunham Massey, *Greater Manchester* (117); Penrhyn Castle, Plas Newydd, *Gwynedd* (107); Knole, *Kent* (103); Wallington, *Northumberland* (119); Nunnington Hall, *North Yorkshire* (119); Powis Castle, *Powys* (107); Angel Corner, *Suffolk* (115); Lacock Abbey, *Wiltshire* (103); Drum Castle, *Grampian* (121); Barrie's Birthplace, *Tayside* (121); Springhill, *Co. Londonderry* (124).

2 *Buried Treasure* (page 6)

Chedworth Roman Villa is in *Gloucestershire*, 5 km (3 miles) NW of Fossebridge, which is on the Cirencester–Northleach road (A429); approach by the Fossebridge–Yanworth–Withington road (NT signposts).

Other Roman sites include Dolaucothi mines, *Dyfed* (107); Segontium, *Gwynedd* (107); Hadrian's Wall and Housesteads Fort, *Northumberland* (119); Letocetum, *Staffordshire* (112); Rough Castle, *Central* (121).

3 *Towers of Strength* (page 8)

Craigievar, Crathes and Drum castles are all in *Grampian*. **Craigievar** is 42 km (26 miles) W of Aberdeen, entry on the W side of A980, 3 km (2 miles) N of the crossroads with A974.

Crathes is 22 km (14 miles) W of Aberdeen and 3 km (2 miles) E of Banchory on A93.

Drum Castle is 16 km (10 miles) W of Aberdeen off A93.

Other towers, castles or mock castles include Clevedon Court, *Avon* (107); Boarstall Tower, *Buckinghamshire* (110); Sizergh Castle, *Cumbria* (117); Castle Drogo, *Devon* (98); Corfe Castle, *Dorset* (98); Cilgerran, *Dyfed* (107); Bodiam, *East Sussex* (103); Skenfrith, *Gwent* (107); Penrhyn, *Gwynedd* (107); Scotney Castle, *Kent* (103); Tattershall Castle, *Lincolnshire* (115); Oxburgh Hall, *Norfolk* (115); Dunstanburgh Castle, *Northumberland* (119); Greys Court, *Oxfordshire* (110); Bramber Castle, *West Sussex* (103); Kellie Castle, *Fife* (121); Brodick

Castle, *Strathclyde* (121); Brodie Castle, Castle Fraser, *Grampian* (121); Castle Ward, *Co. Down* (124); Dunseverick Castle, *Co. Antrim* (124).

4 *The Castle with the Soft Centre* (page 10)

Lindisfarne Castle is in *Northumberland* on Holy Island, 8 km (5 miles) E of Beal across the causeway.

Other converted castles include Chirk, *Clwyd* (107); St Michael's Mount, *Cornwall* (98); Compton, *Devon* (98); Croft, *Hereford and Worcester* (107); Powis, *Powys* (107); Dunster, *Somerset* (98); Baddesley Clinton, *Warwickshire* (112).

5 *Read the Walls* (page 12)

Little Moreton Hall is in *Cheshire*, 6 km (4 miles) SW of Congleton, on E side of A34.

Felbrigg Hall is in *Norfolk*, 3 km (2 miles) SW of Cromer.

Lyveden New Bield is in *Northamptonshire*, 6 km (4 miles) SW of Oundle via A427, 5 km (3 miles) E of Brigstock (A6116) by road from its S end. O.S. Map 141: 983853.

Castle Ward is in *Co. Down*, 11 km (7 miles) NE of Downpatrick, 2 km (1½ miles) W of Strangford.

Other places with striking outside walls include Sudbury Hall, *Derbyshire* (112); Mottisfont Abbey, *Hampshire* (103); Rufford Old Hall, *Lancashire* (117); Speke Hall, *Merseyside* (117); Montacute, *Somerset* (98); Hatchlands, *Surrey* (103); Standen, *West Sussex* (103); East Riddlesden Hall, Nostell Priory, *West Yorkshire* (119).

6 *Save Erddig!* (page 14)

Erddig is in *Clwyd*, 3 km (2 miles) S of Wrexham, off A525.

Other massive restoration projects include Kingston Lacy, *Dorset* (99); Canons Ashby, *Northamptonshire* (112); Beningbrough Hall, *North Yorkshire* (119); Baddesley Clinton, *Warwickshire* (112); Culzean, *Strathclyde* (121); Castle Coole, *Co. Fermanagh* (124).

7 *Long, Dark Evenings* (page 16)

Townend is in *Cumbria*, at S end of Troutbeck village 5 km (3 miles) SE of Ambleside. O.S. Map 90: 407020.

Other homes with no electric light include Little Moreton Hall, *Cheshire* (112); Cotehele, *Cornwall* (99); Knole, *Kent* (103); Springhill, *Co. Londonderry* (125).

8 *Switch on Cragside* (page 18)

Cragside is in *Northumberland*, at Rothbury 26 km (16 miles) NW of Morpeth. Entrance from B6334 only.

Other homes with their own generating plant include Castle Drogo, *Devon* (99); Bateman's, *East Sussex* (103); The Argory, *Co. Tyrone* (125).

9 *Escape from Moseley* (page 20)

Moseley Old Hall is in *Staffordshire*, 6 km (4 miles) N of Wolverhampton, between the Penkridge and Cannock roads just W of A460. O.S. Map 127: 932044.
Other places with escape stories or secret rooms include Little Moreton Hall, *Cheshire* (112); Overbecks, *Devon* (99); Scotney Castle, *Kent* (103); Speke Hall, *Merseyside* (117); Oxburgh Hall, *Norfolk* (115); Coughton Court, Baddesley Clinton, *Warwickshire* (112); Castle Fraser, Craigievar, Crathes, *Grampian* (121); House of The Binns, *Lothian* (121); Castle Ward, *Co. Down* (125).

10 *A Restless Mind* (page 22)

Woolsthorpe Manor is in *Lincolnshire*, 11 km (7 miles) S of Grantham at Colsterworth, just W of A1.
Homes associated with other famous people include Claydon House, *Buckinghamshire* (110); Buckland Abbey, Compton Castle, *Devon* (99); Tŷ Mawr, *Gwynedd* (107); Chartwell, *Kent* (103); George Stephenson's Cottage, *Northumberland* (119); Washington Old Hall, *Tyne and Wear* (119); House of The Binns, *Lothian* (121); Souter Johnnie's Cottage, *Strathclyde* (121).

11 *Word Capsules* (page 24)

Wordsworth House is in *Cumbria* in Cockermouth Main Street.
Homes associated with other famous writers include Hardy's Cottage, *Dorset* (99); Bateman's, *East Sussex* (104); Coleridge Cottage, *Somerset* (99); Bachelors' Club, *Strathclyde* (123); Barrie's Birthplace, *Tayside* (121).

12 *Every Picture Tells a Story* (page 26)

Petworth is in *West Sussex*, 9 km (5½ miles) E of Midhurst, at the junction of A272 and A283.
Other places associated with artists include Saltram, *Devon* (99); Cilgerran, *Dyfed* (107); Dunham Massey, *Greater Manchester* (117); Plas Newydd, *Gwynedd* (107); Mottisfont Abbey, *Hampshire* (104); Flatford Mill, *Suffolk* (115).

13 *Please Don't Touch* (page 28)

Cotehele is in *Cornwall*, on W bank of the Tamar, 13 km (8 miles) SW of Tavistock, 22 km (14 miles) from Plymouth via Saltash Bridge. O.S. Map 201: 422685.
Other serious conservation pressure points include Erddig, *Clwyd* (108); Hill Top, *Cumbria* (117); Hardwick Hall, *Derbyshire* (112); Saltram, *Devon* (99); Knole, *Kent* (104); Uppark, *West Sussex* (104); Craigievar, *Grampian* (121).

14 *Hunt the Ceiling* (page 30)

Knightshayes Court is in *Devon* 3 km (2 miles) N of Tiverton.
Other odd discoveries have been made at Little Moreton Hall, *Cheshire* (112); Penrhyn Castle, *Gwynedd* (108); Castle Fraser, Haddo House, *Grampian* (121, 122); Georgian House, *Lothian* (122); Springhill, *Co. Londonderry* (125).

On the Farm

Working places are fun to explore because there is usually something going on and the link between the past and the present is often clearer if there is some action to see. Old farm buildings built for a special purpose such as storing grain or sheltering animals may still be used today as a tractor shed or a fertilizer store.

In the days of the Saxons, the "barn" was their barley store. Later, as cattle and corn became the main farming products, the barn was used for summer storage and winter threshing. The "threshold" between two opposite and open doors was the place where the wheat sheaves were threshed, or beaten, to separate the corn from the straw. The corn was then "winnowed" in the draught to separate the heavy wheat from the lighter chaff, or outer husk. Today, modern combine harvesters cut and thresh the corn at the same time, but as the corn is often wet, many old barns now house modern, electric grain dryers.

Dovecotes

Imagine trying to store meat without refrigerators and deep freezers. Before the use of winter feeding crops, it was possible to keep only a few animals alive through the winter. All the other animals had to be slaughtered and were salted so that the meat did not go bad. It became boring eating salted food day after day and so dovecotes, or pigeon houses, were built to provide a source of fresh, succulent, tasty meat.

Below: *This pigeon house at Felbrigg is now used by doves. The gardener feeds them and, in return, they eat his apple-tree buds! But they look lovely, sound delightful and provide rich manure droppings.*

Step inside a pigeon house if you have the chance. You will see that it is filled with hundreds of nesting boxes. The pigeons used to feed on the surrounding fields and sleep and nest in their pigeon house. Little did they know that they were going to provide the lord of the manor, who was the only person allowed to own a dovecote, with his fresh supply of meat. A servant would grab an unsuspecting pigeon from its box and, a little later, the mouth-watering smells of pigeon pie would waft from the kitchen to the lord's twitching nose!

Tithe barns

The most spectacular farm buildings of the 13th to 15th centuries were the tithe barns. They were used to store one tenth (a tithe) of each farmer's produce in an area under the control of the Church or the lord of the manor. The idea was to keep a food reserve for the poor or bad times. The roll-in, roll-out sets of doors were designed to allow high-loaded carts to enter through one side of the barn and to leave, unloaded, through the lower doors on the opposite side. The ventilation holes were large enough to keep the building fresh and dry, but small enough to keep out rain and sharp gusts of wind. Sometimes a round owl hole provided access for the resident rat-catcher, the barn owl.

A visit to old, working farm buildings will seldom disappoint you. Automatic milking machines, electric grain dryers, combine harvesters or 70-horse-power tractors can often be seen nestling inside buildings constructed at a time when farmers measured horse power in twos or threes.

The milking stools, lines of men scything hay, and the horses may have long gone but on modern farms new uses can still be found for old buildings carefully erected hundreds of years ago.

Above: *Ashleworth tithe barn was built in about 1500. In this photograph it is of interest to five people: the farmer for storage; the two artists for its beauty; the author for its history; and for you I hope!*

Right: *Old ploughs in the splendid Ardress farm yard, Northern Ireland. For some city children, a school visit is the only way they are likely to see live farm animals.*

Left: *In 1880 this kitchen at Charlecote contained all the latest technology of its time, including the "Prize Kitchener" range at the back left. But what's missing?*

In the Kitchen

Many visitors to country houses find it easier to relate to the "downstairs" work in kitchens than the "upstairs" life of leisure. Even so, you need imagination to help you get the feeling of a hot, bustling kitchen full of bubbling sauces, choppings and slicings, comings and goings.

At first sight the large kitchen *(above)* looks as if it has got almost everything. There are two cooking areas along the back wall, a gleaming set of copper saucepans high on the right and various gadgets on the big table. But look closer.

A place to prepare food

There are no chairs. There is no running water. And there are no food storage cupboards. Far from being a cosy room where meals were cooked and eaten, this was a food preparation room where Cook ruled a staff of fifteen. And you did not sit. Meat was prepared, or dressed, on the central "dresser". Water was carried from the hand-pump in the scullery in large, heavy pots. Here the potato man did nothing but clean potatoes in spring water. Here, too, dishes were washed. Food was *never* left out. The mice and cockroaches were bad enough without temptations of that sort. There were no tins, packets or frozen foods. Instead, there were four rooms where bulk food was stored under the butler's lock and key. There was a dry store for grain, a still room for bottled pickles and fruits, a fish store, and a dairy where milk was churned into butter and cheese.

In 1880, the cooking was done on a brand new, coal-fired "Prize Kitchener" range *(back left)* which had three ovens and four huge

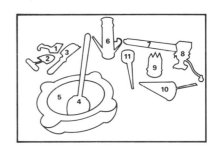

Right: 1 *Vegetable chopper.* 2 *Vegetable slicer with rolling action.* 3 *Meat chopper.* 4 *Pestle and* 5 *Mortar for crushing herbs and spices.* 6 *Coffee percolator.* 7 *Giant rolling pin for pastry.* 8 *Meat mincer.* 9 *"Castle" jelly mould.* 10 *Beer muller. The cone was filled with beer and warmed, or mulled, in the embers of a fire.* 11 *Guess? The handle is hollow with holes at both ends. The answer is on page 64.*

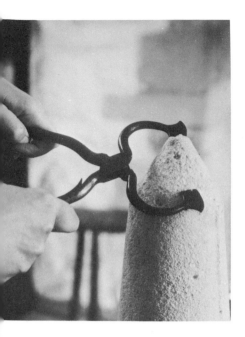

hot plates. To the right, the old hearth was still used but a wood fuel crisis in the 1850s meant that coal was becoming the fuel of the future and the closed range was more efficient because it conserved heat.

The old open hearth at Charlecote was kept in use so that whole sheep and deer could be roasted on the spit in front of the large fire. The rising heat turned a smoke vane in the chimney and by a series of cogs and chains this automatically turned the sizzling meat on the spit at a slow, steady pace. Before the invention of this gadget a small boy used to sit by the fire and turn the spit by hand.

Labour-saving gadgets

All our kitchens have gadgets. From potato peelers and pastry rollers to mincers and jelly moulds, there are easily recognisable gadgets in kitchens which are 100 years old. Charlecote is no exception.

In front of the open hearth there is a cupboard with plates in it. The back of the cupboard is made of metal. This conducted the heat from the open fire and warmed the inside of the cupboard. The whole plate-warming device is on a set of rollers and when loaded with dishes of food and plates, it was pushed along the cold, stone corridor to the dining room where the plates and food were kept hot.

Have a look below at some of the other labour-saving gadgets which bubbled and chopped and sliced their way through life in a kitchen over 100 years ago.

Above: *Most old kitchens will have a pair of sugar cutters which were used for breaking pieces of sugar off the "cone" in the days before packets and boxes of granulated, caster, icing and cubed sugar.*

Out Shopping...

The earliest shops were people's homes. The butcher, the baker, the candlestick maker, or anyone else who had anything to sell, would do so from his own front room or from a stall outside his home.

Certainly in Coggeshall in 1510, the house of Thomas Paycocke was the place to shop . . .

. . . for cloth

Thomas was a rich cloth merchant who, in 1505, built himself a fine timber-framed house in which he wove and sold cloth. His business was so successful that when he died he was able to leave enough money for the poor of Coggeshall for a very long time. This is what is written on his grave:

> "Here lyeth buried Thomas Paycocke who departed this lyfe the XXVIth day of December 1580 and left behind him two daughters Johan and Anne which Thomas Paycocke dydd gyve cc pounds to buy land for the continuall relief of the poore of Coxall *for ever.*"

The £200 ("cc pounds") was used to buy some land which provided income to buy the poor a red or white herring and a bundle of firewood once a year. Four hundred years later the Paycocke charity provides about 25 less well-off people with about £8 a year.

Market Halls are another type of old shop and if you had lived in Winster in 1700, Saturday was the best day to shop . . .

. . . for meat and cheese

No-one knows much about this old Derbyshire building in the middle of Winster High Street, except that the arches used to be

Above: *Paycocke's lies on the busy A120 Harwich docks road and would have collapsed long ago from thundering lorries if it had not been constructed with so much timber. The wood allows the building to shudder without breaking.*

Below: *The Winster market house is still used today as a garage and for storage space for the local VG store.*

open and that on Market Day the whole street was lined with stalls and filled with cattle, horses and jostling crowds. In 1906, the little building was in a terrible condition but was restored by local people who gave it to the National Trust.

Another interesting shop can be found in Edinburgh. In 1632, John Riddoch's was the place to go shopping . . .

. . . for luxuries

Riddoch rented the shop from Thomas Gledstanes who had made several improvements to the Land, or high-storey building. Life was cramped and messy. Everyone lived on top of each other and at night you would have heard people shouting "Gardyloo" as they threw their rubbish and water out of their windows. A pig in the shop survived on these titbits. In this unlikely place Riddoch sold luxury items like prunes, ginger, raisins and rice as well as paper, candles and silk.

Transport and communications were difficult and another long 200 years had to pass before it was possible to ask . . .

. . . for a one penny postage stamp

The Letter Receiving Office of Tintagel opened in a converted manor house four years after Sir Rowland Hill started the Penny Post in 1840. The Cornish village was a popular resort, famous for its legends of King Arthur, and the coming of the railway brought hotels, shops, and more houses to Tintagel.

By 1900, the Old Post Office itself had become threatened by development but a group of local artists saved it in 1903. Today, it squats defiantly hugging the ground. Its roof hangs like a limp washing line and its walls bulge crazily.

Above: "Gardez l'eau" – watch the water at Gladstone's Land. You can still buy candles made here and in summer you may even see a pig in the shop!

Below: Tintagel Old Post Office. No stamps today, but a box in the wall. Just as well it is not on a busy lorry route.

Sit Still!

Classrooms of elementary schools, 100 years ago, were cold and books were rare. Everything was written down on slates with a slate pencil. Each child had a single slate which they had to wipe after every lesson. And every lesson had to be learned by heart, or else you were in trouble.

When exercise books began to be used, an "ink monitor" mixed ink powder with water and the older children wrote with steel-nibbed pens which they dipped into their own ink wells. Writing like this was often a messy business and if you blotted your copybook with a smudge, you started again. The teacher used a blackboard and chalk and helped the children with their mathematics by using an abacus which consisted of rows of coloured beads on wires. Another popular resource was the object-lesson box which contained things that the teacher used as a base to a lesson.

Children ranging from the ages of five to twelve were taught in the same room and sometimes older children helped the teacher by looking after, and even teaching, the younger ones. The class was divided into forms, or benches, with the younger children at the front and the oldest at the back. The best pupils sat at the top of their form on the right. There were no games.

The girls did a lot of needlework and writing was taught by endless copying of words. Everything had to be exactly right. Every "t" had to be crossed and every "i" had to be dotted. Such was school and teaching 100 years ago. But discipline was something quite different.

Right: *Sitting in history. The school room at Sudbury is only opened for school visits. Adults have to look through the glass partition.*

Left: *Once you have learned your lesson, you can wipe your slate clean.*

Below: *A budding teacher gets in some practice.*

40

Discipline

Discipline was strict – very strict. The cane and edge-on rulers were used often. Teachers with weak caning arms were sacked. You were caned for talking, fidgeting, being late, forgetting your number tables, making "speling mistackes", and writing with your left hand even though you were left-handed.

Put your hands behind your backs! Sit up straight! Face the front! Be silent!

Each teacher had a wooden signal device which made a clicking sound. Whenever you heard this sound, you stopped whatever you were doing. Instantly!

Or else you would be rapped across the knuckles and, if you cried, you would be rapped again. *So don't!*

When you were not at school you would be working down a mine, or in a factory, or as a nipper in a windmill, or as a chimney sweep. This meant climbing up chimneys and, if you got stuck, a fire was lit. If that failed to move you, nothing would. Your death would be alone, coughing and spluttering in the soot and smoke.

When you reached the age of twelve, you had to go and work full time, day in, day out, month in, month out, year in, year out. Perhaps school wasn't *so* bad?

Windpower

There was a time when windmills were a common sight, perched on top of hills using the power of the wind to grind corn into flour. Artists included them in paintings of the countryside, but *their* windmills were quiet, romantic and calm with white, silent sails. The truth was different.

Windmills were easily toppled if the wind suddenly changed direction and, during periods of frustrating calm, the miller lost valuable time, which meant money. He might then be tempted to make up for lost time by keeping the canvas on the sails in a strengthening wind. If a gale developed, he ran the risk of the mill running away with itself turning faster and faster. Too many sparks from the whizzing mill stones could set fire to the dry, dusty, wooden mill and many disappeared in this way.

The machinery

Inside every mill there is a baffling maze of ladders, ropes, belts and pulleys each designed for a specific purpose. Working machinery breaks and wears out, so windmills contain timber and gadgets from several different centuries. The result is not a perfect, well-designed machine made at the same time. It is a record of how working men struggled to keep the wretched mill operating. Sometimes they used sheer brute force and a lot of swearing, while at other times they came up with ingenious solutions to maddening problems.

That is the secret of a windmill! The main points to look for when you visit one include the mighty brake wheel (1) at the top of the mill. The horizontal windshaft (2) turned the wallower (3) which turned the vertical wallower shaft (4). Via gears and cogs, this spun the massive millstones (5) at 120 revolutions a minute. Finally, do not miss the ingenious governor (6) which controlled the gap between the millstones to match the strength of the wind.

The Nipper

No visit to a windmill is complete without some idea of the Nipper. He was the miller's dogsbody, usually aged between ten and fourteen, and his many jobs included tying the canvas cloth on to the wooden sails. If the brake was not tight enough, the sails would begin to turn as more cloth was unfolded and the Nipper could find himself dangling 6 metres off the ground *upside down*. His job was to dress the sails as fast as possible before climbing into the top of the mill through a little window above the windshaft (7).

His other duties included minding all the unguarded, moving machinery; hauling and hoisting sacks of grain to the top of the mill; sweeping the dusty floors and running errands for his master. He received low pay for his long, hard hours.

Above: *The Pitstone windmill is dated 1627. Fully restored it faces the cement works, another local landmark. I wonder what the cement works will look like in about AD 2340?*

Below: *The magic of windpower is still tempting. These serious ideas for windmills at sea are being floated by the Central Electricity Generating Board.*

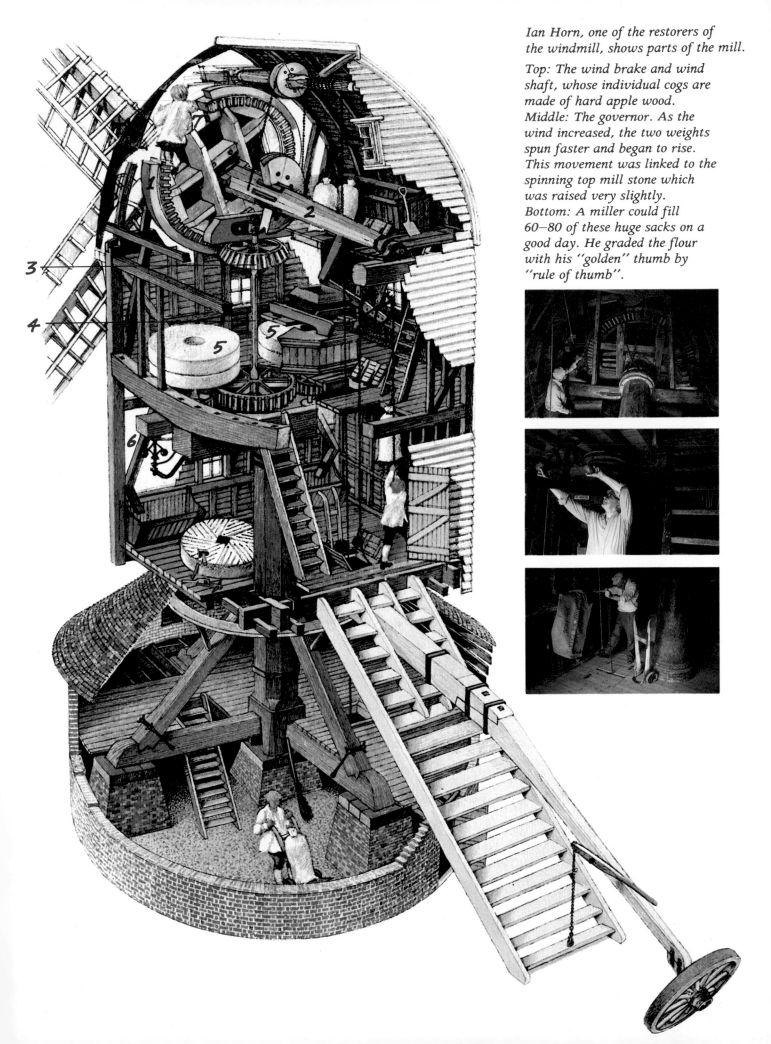

Ian Horn, one of the restorers of the windmill, shows parts of the mill.

Top: The wind brake and wind shaft, whose individual cogs are made of hard apple wood.

Middle: The governor. As the wind increased, the two weights spun faster and began to rise. This movement was linked to the spinning top mill stone which was raised very slightly.

Bottom: A miller could fill 60–80 of these huge sacks on a good day. He graded the flour with his "golden" thumb by "rule of thumb".

The Wellbrook Beetling Mill

One of the most unusual working places in the British Isles must be the mill at Wellbrook in Northern Ireland. Beetling is the last process in the manufacture of linen, which is a type of cloth made out of flax. Today the process is done with modern rollers and presses, but in the past the cloth was pounded by 32 wooden rams which gave it a smooth sheen, or shiny surface. Each ram was called a beetle.

The Wellbrook Mill was powered by a stream which turned a waterwheel. By using a clever system of gears and cogs, the revolving waterwheel turned the pounding machinery every two seconds and the cloth-carrying rollers every 20 minutes. The 32 beetles were raised and lowered one after the other in such a way that there were only 7 beetles pounding the cloth at any one time.

This ingenious system worked 24 hours a day, 6 days a week from 1765 until 1965. There were breakdowns but never for very long because lost time meant lost pay.

Full restoration

When the mill closed in 1965, it quickly began to rot and that would have been the end of Wellbrook if people had not decided to save it. In 1968, work began on restoring the mill to full working order. With the help and skills of the last beetler, William John Black, and the last millwright, Albert Pogue, Wellbrook once again vibrates to the incredible thump, thump, thump, thump of its pounding beetles.

Above: *Every four seconds, one after the other, each beetle is raised and then dropped on to the slow-turning roll of cloth below. The sight and noise has to be seen and heard to be believed.*

The large handle at the top turns the water power on and off.

The job of the beetler

William John Black watched his father at work when he was nine years old and began working himself in the mill when he was fourteen. His long apprenticeship finally allowed him to beetle his own cloth when he was 25.

Many things could go wrong.

The cloth had to be absolutely straight on the beam otherwise a crease would develop. A beetled crease was one that could not be "un-beetled" and the cloth would be ruined.

If the beetles were moving too quickly, they did not touch the cloth and so did not produce a sheen. If they moved too slowly, they could leave an unwanted mark on the precious material. Everything had to be just right.

Water was sprayed on the cloth to help give it the sheen, but if dyes were being used and too much water was added, the dyes would run and that would mean another ruined product.

In autumn, fallen leaves could block the outside grill and stop the water flow, and that could lose a night's beetling and a night's pay. Worst of all, if a stick somehow got through the grill and lodged between one of the waterwheel buckets, it could throw out the line of the wheel and that meant costly repairs and loss of beetling time.

No scarves or loose clothing were allowed in the mill. If anything got caught in the machinery it could cost the beetler his life. One man was hung on his own scarf and another lost his head in the wiper beam. This was the most dangerous part of the mill because the wipers turned *inwards* and there was no time to escape their deadly revolutions.

Without the fully restored Wellbrook Mill, it would be impossible to understand the work and machines of the beetler.

Above: *The beetling engine consists of a revolving wiper beam with 32 wipers bolted on to it. Each beetle has a shaft through the middle of it. As the wiper beam revolves (anti-clockwise) the wipers raise the shafts on the beetles which then fall on to the cloth, one after the other. William John Black at the age of 73. The last beetler of Wellbrook.*

Left: *Diagram of the mill showing all seven beetling engines.*
1. *Water from stream carried in raised trough*
2. *Water wheel*
3. *Beetling "engine"*
4. *Beetles*
5. *Cloth on roller beam*
6. *Wiper beam*
7. *Wipers*
8. *Gears and cogs*

Remember that the men who built Wellbrook had no books, plans or computers to help them. They started with a field next to a stream. . . .

Beauty and the Beast

Imagine you knew a secret way of melting metals out of special rocks called ores. Better still, imagine how you would feel if you had discovered a way of melting, or smelting, good quality metal, such as copper, out of poor quality ores.

Ulrich Frosse, a German copper smelter, was in such a position in 1584. He had been encouraged to work in Britain by Queen Elizabeth I who realised that the ability to smelt metal would be very important to Britain.

Frosse worked at a secret location called Aberdulais in South Wales. It was a small, beautiful, natural hollow with a waterfall on one side. Nearby hills covered in trees and containing many coal seams, provided wood, and then coal, to heat the ores to the right temperatures.

In July 1585 Frosse wrote,

"We have found out a way to melt 24 hundredweight of ore every day with one furnace ... we will melt with two furnaces in 40 weeks, 560 tonnes of ore."

Within two years Frosse made his dramatic breakthrough when he discovered a way of using poor as well as good quality ore. Suddenly the supplies of ore from Cornwall and Europe became urgent. On 7 March 1587, Frosse wrote:

"Send such ores as you have with much speed as may not caring what ore it is. Send of all sorts the better it will melt and with more profit ..."

But Aberdulais was never to become a giant industrial complex. There was no room for it to develop within its little hollow. Instead, it became a kind of research centre which pioneered ways of smelt-

Top and above: *Ever-changing Aberdulais, today and in 1816.*
"Among these scenes,
the memory strays,
Scenes of life's
Far earlier days ....
Much alter'd now
The scene appears;
And trade its busy
Form uprears;
Where silence reigned,
Now tumult rings;
So change is marked
On human things."
William Young, miller at Aberdulais 1797–1802.

ing copper, iron and tin. Despite all this industrial activity, Aberdulais never lost its natural beauty. It was the nearby towns of Swansea and Port Talbot that saw giant developments of steel and tin-plate industries which have shaped our lives so dramatically.

Over the years, Aberdulais once again became a secret hollow, tucked away and out of sight. By 1978, it was a rubbish tip.

Forging a community

The massive metal industries that developed in South Wales as a result of the secret of Aberdulais forged a fiercely independent people who for generations have toiled in the mighty steelworks and have worked down coal mines to provide power for the hungry furnaces. They still do.

In the 1900s boys aged between eight and fourteen were told to urinate on their hands to toughen them up. They wore wooden non-heat-conducting clogs on cobbled floors. Around their necks and scrawny, glistening bodies they wore towels to absorb their sweat and drank salt water to replace lost sodium. Leather aprons were worn for protection from the liquid, molten metals, and baths of cold water hissed as hot tongs were dipped repeatedly to keep them just cool enough to hold.

It all started at Aberdulais and in 1981 a project to restore the site was begun. Working, sweating men can never be re-created on site but the rubbish has been cleared and each stone of the remaining arches and foundations has been made safe. A waterwheel will shortly provide an industrial, regulated sound to match the natural pourings of the waterfall.

The sound of the ever-flowing water and the remains of cobbled floors, arches and channels fire the imagination, which is why Aberdulais is such a special place of beauty *and* historic worth.

Above: *Restoration, stone by numbered stone.*

Below: *Steel mills of today can produce 300 tonnes of steel in 20 minutes.*

Restoring Styal

The Industrial Revolution of the 18th century was founded on iron and steel. New machines swept away old ways of doing things. Factories were built and people moved from the countryside into rapidly growing cities.

Spinning and weaving crafts changed dramatically because of inventors and inventions that have now become history-book names. The Spinning Jenny; Hargreaves; Arkwright; and Compton's Spinning Mules meant in their time the death of home-spun cloth and the birth of factory products spun and woven on machines. And who was to work these new machines? Once again, it was the children who did the nastier jobs. Their little hands could oil parts that adults could not reach and by quickly crawling under the machinery they could piece together a snapped cotton yarn in their nimble fingers.

The moving parts on the Spinning Mule, in particular, had to be watched carefully. A child would walk an average of 40 miles (64 km) a day backwards and forwards watching the endless to-ing and fro-ing of the relentless machinery and the valuable threads. Samuel Greg founded a new factory mill at Styal in 1784 and used the River Bollin to turn a huge waterwheel which powered the new machines. His great-great-grandson gave the mill to the Trust in 1939 and cloth was produced there until 1959.

Spinning and weaving courses

In 1977, the Quarry Bank Trust was set up to restore and develop the mill as a living museum of the textile industry. Today, there are demonstrations of spinning and weaving and a waterwheel is being installed to power the rows of machines once again. The mill is a place to learn old crafts of spinning and weaving during popular weekend and day courses.

Below: *Some young workers involved in the massive project to restore Quarry Bank Mill.*

Left: *A school group watches a hand-spinning demonstration at the start of a tour round the mill. A Spinning Jenny stands on the right.*

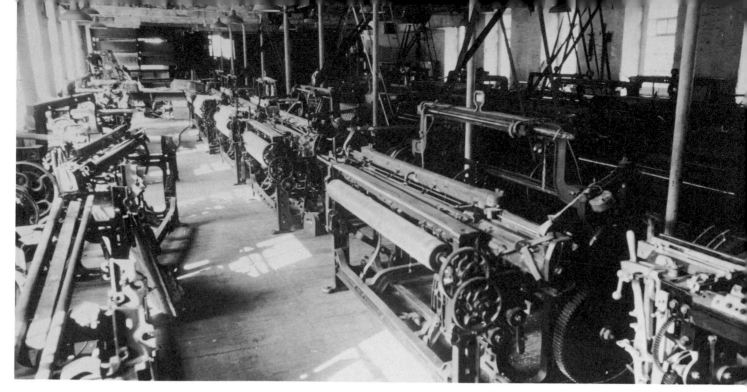

Life at the mill

The restoration of the mill and a chance to work some of its machinery will help children of today understand the lives of some of the children of the past.

Between the ages of nine and eighteen, they worked a 13-hour day, six days a week in return for food, clothing and a roof over their heads. The hours, from 6 am until 7 pm allowed only ten minutes for breakfast and half an hour for dinner. The children slept together two to a bed (sheets were changed once a month) in the Apprentice House which had space for 100 children. It might come as a shock, therefore, to know that Styal was thought to be one of the most forward-looking mills in the country which offered some of the *best* conditions of its time.

Above: *Lines of weaving looms at Samuel Greg's Quarry Bank Mill at Styal, Cheshire.*

Above: *Oak cottages, built in the 1820s and lived in by descendants of the mill workers today. The school at the end of the row is still used by Styal children.*

The Styal community

Samuel Greg was one of the first mill owners to employ a medical officer, Mr Holland, to keep a check on the children's health. He also provided a teacher, John Thornton, to teach the basic skills of reading, writing and arithmetic, and in 1788 he even employed a music teacher.

Classes were held each Sunday and on one weekday evening. As the mill prospered, more workers were needed and so Greg built cottages for them in the 1820s. When the children reached eighteen, they moved from the Apprentice House to lodgings in the cottages – usually in the basement.

Later, if they married, they were able to rent cottages which had a parlour, back kitchen, two bedrooms and an outside toilet (called a privy). Each cottage also had its own small plot for growing vegetables.

A village shop was opened and eventually run by the workers themselves as a profit-sharing business. Today the shop has closed but Styal village remains an active, lived-in place.

Preserving Lacock

Lacock is another village which is owned by the Trust but it is very different from Styal. Instead of being built all at the same time as a planned, industrial village, Lacock has grown, adapted and changed over hundreds of years. And yet there is a connection between the two villages.

Lacock grew in the 14th and 15th centuries as a wealthy centre for the weaving of cloth which was homespun in upstairs rooms by hand. This continued until the Industrial Revolution when the Samuel Gregs of the world began to change things. Cottage weaving in Lacock died out in the 1830s just at the time when Greg was building uniform cottages for his growing number of factory workers at Styal. From that moment, Lacock was doomed as a working village able to support itself.

Spot the difference!

The village was owned by the Talbot family from the time of Henry VIII until 1944 when Matilda Talbot gave Lacock to the Trust. Since then many of the shops have gone although the buildings remain. Apart from this, the village looks much the same as it did 100 years ago. Why is this? Have a look at the top photograph on the right. It is the village High Street, but what is missing? Try and name at least five ordinary things which you would expect to see in a village street. What makes it look different?

An inside job

The Trust wanted to preserve the outside of the interesting and varied houses while at the same time it had to cope with the coming of electricity and television.

Careful planning has meant that electricity cables and telephone wires have been buried underground. Television signals are piped to the houses by cable rather than by ugly rooftop aerials. There are no double yellow parking lines, or street signs, or illuminated advertising signs. There is not even a pavement down the main street — instead the road goes right up to the houses as it did in the days before motor cars. There are no concrete street lamps to flood the village in yellow easy-to-drive-in light. Lacock looks much the same as it did *before* all the modern lamps, wires, cables, signs, and regulations of our time.

But the village is far from dead. The insides of many of the houses have been fully modernised and are rented to local people who know the area and who work nearby.

By owning the *whole* village the Trust has been able to preserve the special variety of buildings that have been adapted and altered over hundreds of years. It is as if the houses have nudged and jostled each other, rubbing shoulders and wriggling, until finally they have settled into a line that looks "right".

Top: *Lacock High Street. Can you name at least five things you would expect to see in an ordinary street which are missing from here?*

Middle left: *The telephone box is painted grey so that it blends better with the buildings.*

Middle right: *The old smithy, where horses were shod by the blacksmith, is now the bus shelter.*

Bottom left: *A line of cars are parked outside the village school.*

Bottom right: *More repairs to a line of houses that have different roof angles, windows and materials but which somehow look "right".*

50

Cornish Engines

It is rare to own and preserve *whole* villages such as Lacock, but it is often possible to preserve one particular building or feature within a village. This is certainly the case at Pool in Cornwall half-way between Camborne and Redruth. Two buildings stand out head and shoulders above the rest.

Pumping engines

Cornwall used to be an important mining area which supplied tin to the smelting industry of South Wales. The problem was that the deep mines kept flooding and so water had to be pumped out of them day and night.

In the early 1800s, a Cornishman, Richard Trevithick, invented a high-pressure steam engine which revolutionised the pumping of water out of the mines. This is how it worked: super-heated "strong steam", as Trevithick called it, was produced in a high-pressure boiler. Then it was passed into a cylinder, where the combination of expanding high-pressure steam at the top of the cylinder and contracting, or condensing, steam at the bottom was enough to move the piston downwards. The piston was attached to one end of a mighty rocking beam called a "bob". The other end of the bob was attached to the top of the pumping rod.

As the piston moved *down*, so it rocked the bob which pulled *up* the rod. Then the weight of the falling rod pulled *down* on the bob which raised the piston back *up* to its starting position. On each "stroke" up and down, the rod reached all the way to the bottom of the mine. It was made up of about 30 lengths of wood *each* measuring *20 metres* bolted end to end.

Right at the bottom of the rod, 600 metres down, there was a plunger which sucked up the water in the same way as a water pistol is filled. Because of the weight of air pressing down on the earth, it

Left: *The pumping engine at Taylor's shaft.*

Above: *The East Pool winding engine, or "whim", was used to raise and lower cages in the mine shaft.*

Right: *Diagrammatic view of how the water was pumped up the shaft. The drawing shows the same engine but in two positions – the "upstroke" and "downstroke". On the upstroke the water is being sucked out of each of the tanks (1). All the plungers (2) are raised and all the top valves (3) are closed.*

On the downstroke the lower valves (4) are now closed, the plunger moves down and this pushes the water through the now-open top valves and up into the tanks.

The filled tanks are then ready to be sucked dry on the next upstroke – and so on for years on end!

Note that the diagram shows less than half of the full length of the pump.

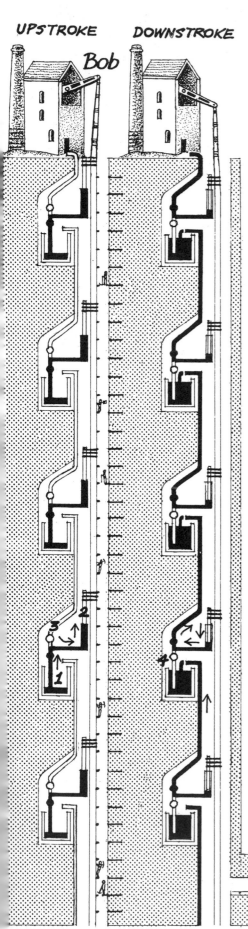

UPSTROKE **DOWNSTROKE**

Bob

is only possible, by suction, to raise water 9.8 metres at a time, and so there was a series of tanks and plungers all the way up the shaft, sucking up water in columns 9.8 metres long. These giant engines were able to pump 2,052 litres of water a *minute* out of the mine and the total weight of moving water was about 80 tonnes.

Taylor's shaft

By 1860, there were 650 pumping engines working day and night pumping water out of Cornish tin mines, but at the turn of the century, mines in the United States and Australia began to be developed and the Cornish industry collapsed. By 1925, there were just 20 engines still working and the very last engine to be built was at Taylor's shaft in East Pool.

It began work in 1925 pumping water at the rate of 121,000 litres an hour, day in, day out for 20 continuous years. When the mine closed in 1945, there were plans to scrap the old engine but flooding overtook another part of the mine, and so the engine was started again for another nine years. Finally, when diesel replaced steam, her work came to a rest when the engine staff shut down the boiler at 11.30 am on 28 September 1954. An American, Mr Greville Bath, bought and saved her from the scrap heap. She dominates the skyline of Pool to this day.

Getting to work . . . and back

Working down the mine was hard and dangerous and in the early years the men used to ride on the moving rod in order to get up and down the mine. There were little steps on the rod at 2.7 metre intervals and corresponding platforms at the side of the shaft. As the rod began its upward flight, a miner would step on to it and ride up 2.7 metres. Then he stepped off on to a platform and waited while the rod moved downwards on its "down stroke" before stepping on once again and riding up on the next "up stroke". Imagine doing that 200 times! Later, miners were moved in cages which were wound up and down the mine by winding engines called "whims". Even these were not always very safe as the following story shows.

One of the drivers had not been watching the indicator showing the position of the cage and he suddenly realised that it was heading at full speed for the top of the shaft. There were only seconds to go – certainly no time to apply the brake and shut off steam – so he slammed the engine into reverse. This broke all the gearing but stopped the cage instantly just a metre from the top of the winding wheel. The men bowed their heads in prayer for a few moments and then set off for the engine house and its quivering driver where all hell let loose! After that, it was time for a long, steady drink.

Out for a Drink

The Fleece Inn

Lola Taplin was born in the Fleece Inn and lived there all her life. She ran it by herself for 30 years until she died in 1977 at the age of 83.

Her pub was her home. She put vases of flowers on the tables and kept her own furniture and knick-knacks in the rooms. She did not allow peanuts, posters or crisps in her homely pub and accepted beer only if it was delivered in wooden barrels.

She was convinced that evil spirits haunted the Fleece and so she painted white circles under the chimney in order to keep them out.

She left her pub to the National Trust on condition that her furniture remained in the same place, that crisps and peanuts would never be served and that the stone floors would remain uncarpeted. The white circles were to be chalked regularly and flowers should be on the table. And that is how it is!

The Tyn-y-Groes Hotel

This Welsh hotel was once a coaching inn where tired horses were changed for fresh ones in the days before cars and buses. The inn was the centre of the local farming community and even today, farm rents are paid twice a year in one of the bars. The hotel is in a part of the Dolmelynllyn estate which was first given to the Trust in 1924. It is a perfect centre for a holiday in North Wales with fishing, swimming, superb waterfalls, pony trekking, Snowdon and even gold mines, nearby.

Above: *White lines and flowers. No carpets, posters and crisps. Lola Taplin's Fleece Inn at Bretforton continues business as usual.*

Below: *The old coaching inn of Tyn-y-Groes refreshes people rather than horses today.*

The Bachelors' Club

In 1780, a 21-year-old son of a farmer formed a club near Ayr with his bachelor friends. Here they talked, drank, sang and generally enjoyed themselves. The young man was Robert Burns and in his head were jigs, songs, rhymes and poems that were to make him Scotland's best-loved poet. Membership of the Club was limited to
"any cheerful honest-hearted lad, who, if he has a friend that is true, and a mistress that is kind, and as much wealth as genteely to make both ends meet – is just as happy as this world can make him ..."
Their first debate was whether a man should marry for looks or money!
Every year, a local Burns' society meets in the Club to celebrate the poet's birth with whisky and haggis.

Above:
"What is title? what is treasure?
What is reputation's care?
If we lead a life of pleasure,
'Tis no matter how or where!

A fig for those by law protected!
Liberty's a glorious feast!
Courts for cowards were erected,
Churches built
to please the priest."
*From "The Jolly Beggars"
by Robert Burns.*

Below: *Gaslight and Guinness at The Crown, Belfast.*

The Crown Liquor Saloon

In the 1880s, Mr Flanagan of The Crown in Belfast, visited Spain and Italy and was so impressed by the colourful wine bars that he decided to cheer up his father's dreary pub. He employed church craftsmen from Dublin and Italy to let their skills loose on the pub, and the result is fabulous. There are snug boxes, like old church pews, around the walls and drinks are ordered by pressing a bell-push. This moves a lettered disc on the far wall which alerts the barmen. On Saturday mornings, the butcher delivers meat which is lined up along the back wall of the bar. These are the joints that have been ordered by husbands who have told their wives that they are just popping out to buy the Sunday joint.

Places of Worship

I N NORTHERN IRELAND on the Londonderry coast, a temple perches on the edge of a high cliff. It sits silently within earshot of the timeless sea and circling gulls. From here, the man who built it looked out across the vast ocean which inspired him so much and thanked God for its beauty.

Frederick Hervey was the Protestant Bishop of Londonderry in the 1780s. He was a popular, kind-hearted man who did much to improve church buildings. He added a spire to his own cathedral in Londonderry which still dominates the city and he helped towards the cost of building Roman Catholic chapels. He treated all religious faiths with equal respect and at a time when local Catholics were badly persecuted, he invited them to celebrate Mass in the crypt of his cliff-top temple. His far-sighted tolerance was an act of faith in a God who meant as much to Catholics as to Protestants.

I N SCOTLAND the island and Abbey of Iona have drawn thousands of pilgrims from all over the world for hundreds of years. It is like a spiritual battery that restores energy to people working with the Church in difficult and deprived places. The links with Glasgow are particularly strong after the Reverend George Macleod restored the Abbey in 1938 and founded the Iona Community of active, working Christians. Iona has been a sacred site since the landing of St Columba in AD 563 and a sense of peace and calm fills the island. There are no cars. No coaches. Just a street and a huge working Abbey on a tiny island.

Someone once wrote that the veil between Heaven and Earth is very thin on Iona. Don't ever miss a chance of visiting this extra-ordinary place. You will never regret it.

Above: *The Mussenden Temple. Named after Bishop Hervey's cousin Mrs Mussenden and completed in 1785.*

The Latin words around the dome mean: " 'Tis pleasant safely to behold from shore the rolling ship, and hear the tempest roar."

Left: "Behold Iona!
A blessing on each
eye that see-eth it."
St Columba AD 563

Right: *Sandham Memorial Chapel. Spencer's painted scenes of everyday life in World War I include floor scrubbing, bedmaking, map reading, sorting the laundry and kit inspection. The faces of the soldiers tell the misery of their war.*

IN ENGLAND the Sandham Memorial Chapel reflects the horror of war and its effect on one man, Stanley Spencer. As a young man he served in World War I and made notes and sketches of his ghastly experiences. When he returned, he vowed to paint a chapel in memory of the men who had died. It took him five years to paint the scenes that had been forged by experience on to his memory, and the powerful paintings are a reminder of the horror of wars.

IN WALES Tŷ Mawr is the birthplace of Bishop Morgan who, in 1578, began a translation of the Bible into Welsh. It took him ten years to write but the result was an easy-to-read version of the Bible which probably saved the Welsh language. At that time there were very few books in Welsh and William Morgan's translation came at just the right moment.

Two hundred years later, a 16-year-old girl called Mary Jones walked 26 miles (42 km) barefoot to buy a Welsh Bible. Her story led to the founding of the British Bible Society in 1804. Today the Society distributes over 10 million Bibles a year to countries all over the world. This has led to the translation of the New Testament into 795 different languages.

Right: *Tŷ Mawr. Despite its humble appearance, it is renowned as the birthplace of the translator of the Bible into Welsh, Bishop William Morgan.*

Ar y dde: *Tŷ Mawr. Er ei olwg distadl mae'n dŷ enwog am mai dyma fan geni'r Esgob William Morgan, cyfiethydd y Beibl i'r Gymraeg.*

The Fishermen of Carrick-a-Rede

As a boy, Pat Donnelly watched his father put up the fishermen's rope bridge at Carrick-a-Rede. He in turn has passed on his knowledge to Sean Morton and, between them, they have been responsible for the bridge for over 40 years.

A lunging 18-metre wide, 25-metre deep chasm separates the fishermen on the coast from their salmon nets on the small island and every spring they bridge the gap with skills and knowledge passed down for over 250 years. Pat says:

"It's a storm that really tests her. It's really desperate, you know. I've seen the planks being lifted as high as the ropes and then come crashing down on the wires in the gusting wind. It can be bucking like a horse. I crossed it once with a fishing rod doubling around me, you know. I had a salmon in one hand and my rod in the other with the wind blowin' and tearin' and I was glad to be off her, I can tell you!"

The bridge is checked every day of the fishing season, which lasts from April until September. During warm weather, the ropes have to be tightened to keep the bridge straight and taut. In wet weather the fishermen slacken the ropes to stop them tightening the bridge to breaking point.

It is comforting to know about Pat and Sean and their young team when you cross their bridge alone. Way below you the sea heaves and thuds a cavernous tune. Above, the seagulls mockingly laugh at you. And in front, 18 metres of plank and rope silently beckon, "Come on, I dare you!"

Above: *75-year-old Pat Donnelly jokes with Sean Morton after putting up the bridge for another season.*

Carrick-a-Rede is on Northern Ireland's Antrim coast. The name means "the rock on the road" – the road being the path of salmon on their way north.

58

Top: *The men who first bridged Carrick-a-Rede over 250 years ago used their knowledge of sailing tackle to help them. Today, block and tackle equipment is used in the same way, and so are the original tethering holes.*

The heavy bridge is paid out from the same side that the men are pulling from. This means that they pull it across straight and level and avoid having to haul a heavy, sagging weight.

Middle: *From father to son, the skill is passed on. 54-year-old Sean Morton stands at the far end while his 21-year-old son, Sean, tightens a chain on the mainland. "Toots" inspects the work but decides against jumping. Pat brings the last two planks.*

Bottom: *The fishermen's skill provides them with access to the salmon and us with a bridge worth experiencing.*

It bounces as you walk on it and the first crossing leaves you shaking the other side. Then you have to cross back. Pat tells a good story of an airline pilot who after two attempts failed to cross the bridge at Carrick-a-Rede.

New Uses for Old Buildings

From the humble . . .

The little house on the right sits over Stock Ghyll in Ambleside, Cumbria, as it has done for over 400 years. Floods and road planners have not affected Bridge House, and its cheeky position has surprised visitors to Ambleside for many years.

It was built in the early 1500s as a crossing over the beck and as a store for apples. Later, in the 1700s, a fireplace and chimney were added and it was lived in for a time by several different folk.

By 1817, it had become a tea-room and a small weaving shop; in 1843, it was occupied by "Chairy" Rigg who repaired chairs and lived in the house with his wife and *six* children! In 1905, a cobbler used the bottom half of the house as his repair shop and the top half as a pigeon loft. He was followed by another cobbler called Collingworth who kept his leather upstairs.

Then Bridge House became an antiques "olde gift shoppe" and finally, in 1926, it was bought for £450 by local people who gave it to the Trust. And so here it stands as an information centre for the Trust in the Lake District. Despite its humble appearance that little roof has seen quite a lot.

Today it is easy for us to demolish old buildings and build a new world of concrete and glass. If that happened throughout the country, we would lose a great deal more than just buildings. We would lose stories and oddities and a sense of history that is easy to understand. We can chuckle at the thought of "Chairy" Rigg and his large family in Bridge House, or cry in a room where a baby once died. Buildings link us with people who lived, loved and died hundreds of years before us. In a nuclear age that can be a comforting link.

Above: *Bridge House, Ambleside. Some say it was built over the ghyll to avoid the payment of ground rent.*

Left: *The village of Culross, Scotland, provides such a perfect setting that it is hired frequently by television companies and film crews for historical films and programmes.*

. . . to the more extravagant

The Guildhall in Lavenham, Suffolk, was built at much the same time as Bridge House and its life has been just as varied. The Guild of Corpus Christi built it and controlled the sale of wool from within it. Church festivals and processions were also held in the Guildhall, but after Henry VIII's *Reformation* of the Church, the hall was used more as a social centre than as a religious place.

In 1555, the Rector of Hadleigh, Dr Rowland Taylor, was kept a prisoner at the hall before being burned at the stake for his religious beliefs.

Then the Guildhall became the Town Hall of Lavenham, but after 80 years or so it was used as a public prison. A pillory, whipping post and stocks stood outside the hall whose walls were in such a bad state that the prisoners were secured by their thumbs to prevent them escaping.

Almost 100 years later, it became a workhouse and then an almshouse for the poor. During World War II, it was used by evacuees from London and for a while it was also a restaurant and then became a nursery school.

It was given to the Trust in 1951 and local people collected money for essential repairs. Today its contribution to Lavenham remains as a place for a local history collection and as a centre for public meetings and social events.

Below: *The Guildhall, Lavenham*.

Fair Isle

Crouching alone in an October gale on top of Malcolm's Head is a sure way of convincing anyone that Fair Isle is indeed Britain's most remote inhabited island.

Lines of black, hail curtains thunder towards you from a white-tossed sea forcing you to turn the other cheek. They thud into your billowing anorak like demons possessed and demand that you kneel on to at least one knee.

Far below you, over edges that you dare not seek, the mighty cliffs plunge vertically to a cauldron of froth and spume that hurls itself endlessly at the cliffs. As each curtain passes, the reassuring crofts of the islanders appear in great shafts of fast-moving sunlight. That is Fair Isle – wild and beautiful and home to 70 people.

Above: *View from Malcolm's Head. "Bailey, Fair Isle. Westerly severe gale Force 9 imminent backing Storm Force 10 later in Fair Isle."*

Just right for dumping the old vans (centre top cliff). *One push and the raging sea will pound them to pieces without trace. The island is only 3½ miles (6 km) from north to south and about 1½ miles (2 km) wide.*

Life on the island

Below: *Over the cliff go the heads and entrails of eight island sheep.*

Little everyday things confirm how tough life can be on the island. Every porch is crammed with gumboots and steaming, bright yellow oilskins. Each croft has a web of clothes lines, criss-crossed to cater for every possible wind direction. The Chapel door is locked, not against vandals but to prevent the wind bursting open the door and flooding the aisle with sheets of horizontal rain.

The islanders are virtually self-sufficient. They grow their own vegetables, catch their own fish and lobsters, and rear and slaughter their own sheep. They also have to be prepared to turn a hand to most things from being a coastguard to a carpenter or plumber – or all three.

If an emergency arises, the islanders often have to deal with it alone, especially in the winter when the weather can cut off the island for weeks.

Modern technology

During the early 1950s, the island was dying. Life was too hard and remote for the young people and many left. There is little doubt that Fair Isle, like so many other outer Scottish islands, would have become deserted if the National Trust for Scotland had not bought the island in 1954. Many people and other organisations have been involved in the island's rescue but, in the end, it has been the islanders themselves who have shown that financial help given to them is spent wisely and effectively.

In 1959, a new pier was opened for their boat *The Good Shepherd*. The crofts were gradually rebuilt. Piped water, followed by electricity, was put in during the 1960s. Then came a small airstrip and improved radio communications in the 1970s. In 1981, the islanders built a community hall and finished a sheltered slipway for *The Good Shepherd*, and 1982 saw the introduction of a wind generator for electricity.

Above: The Good Shepherd *slipway, completed in 1981.*

Right: *Annie Thomson* (centre) *with her daughter Anne and grand-daughter Lise, aged eleven. Annie once knitted a jersey for the Duke of Edinburgh in a week.*

"The wires" – knitting Fair Isle style

Modern technology has saved the island and with it a craft that goes back hundreds of years. Although Fair Isle jerseys are known the world over, in 1971 there were just three women on the island who could knit them. One of them, Annie Thomson, made a conscious effort to keep the skill alive by, as she put it, "Taking my wires a bit more seriously."

The result is that 12 women knit regularly and have passed on their skill to their children and grandchildren. The striking patterns and style that they use were born out of a unique community which thanks to the present has saved part of the past for a confident future.

Knitting mind-bogglers:
Lise does not remember learning to knit. Her first product was an egg cosy when she was four. Fair Isle jerseys are knitted as a whole *with no seams. Knitters use up to 5 needles on the same jersey.*

The diamond shapes are equally balanced down the centre of the jersey.

No jersey is ever exactly *the same because no patterns or row numbers are ever written down. Instead they are passed from one generation to the next by word and example.*

The influences on the shapes and patterns go back over 2,000 years via old sea routes of the Vikings, Egyptians and Indians.

All the colours are natural.

The Working Places in Part Two

Where to find them

Directions are given to the nearest kilometre and mile, and include, where relevant, map references based on the 1:50 000 Series of Ordnance Survey maps. After each main entry there is a list of associated places from all over the United Kingdom. Extra details and directions for these are given on the page numbers shown in brackets.

15 *On the Farm* (page 34)

Ashleworth Tithe Barn is in *Gloucestershire*, 10 km (6 miles) N of Gloucester on W bank of the Severn, SE of Ashleworth. O.S. Map 162: 818252.

Felbrigg Hall is in *Norfolk*, 3 km (2 miles) SW of Cromer.

Ardress House is in *Co. Armagh*, 11 km (7 miles) from Portadown on the Moy road (B28).

Other interesting farm buildings or collections include Willington Dovecote, *Bedfordshire* (110); Wimpole Hall, *Cambridgeshire* (115); Tattondale Home Farm, *Cheshire* (112); Erddig, *Clwyd* (108); Buckland Abbey, *Devon* (99); Bredon, Hawford, Middle Littleton, Wichenford, *Hereford and Worcester* (108); Great Coxwell, *Oxfordshire* (110); West Pennard, *Somerset* (99); Shugborough Park Farm, *Staffordshire* (112); Kinwarton Dovecote, *Warwickshire* (112); East Riddlesden Hall, *West Yorkshire* (119); Lacock, *Wiltshire* (104); Pitmedden, Boath, *Grampian* (122); Phantassie, *Lothian* (122); Angus Folk Museum, *Tayside* (122).

16 *In the Kitchen* (page 36)

The answer to the question on page 36: the gadget with the hollow handle that looks like a saucepan was used to fill special hollow-bottomed plates with hot water in order to keep the plates warm. The handle acted as a spout which fitted into a special opening in the plates.

Charlecote Park is in *Warwickshire*, 6 km (4 miles) E of Stratford-upon-Avon, on N side of B4086.

Other interesting kitchens include Clevedon Court, *Avon* (109); Erddig, *Clwyd* (109); Cotehele, Lanhydrock, *Cornwall* (99); Hardwick Hall, *Derbyshire* (113); Castle Drogo, Saltram, *Devon* (99); Dunham Massey, *Greater Manchester* (117); Carlyle's House, *London* (110); Canons Ashby, *Northamptonshire* (113); Cragside, Wallington, *Northumberland* (119); Barrington Court, *Somerset* (99); Clandon Park, *Surrey* (104); Washington Old Hall, *Tyne and Wear* (119); Uppark, *West Sussex* (104); Brodie Castle, *Grampian* (122); Georgian House, Gladstone's Land, *Lothian* (122); Brodick Castle, *Strathclyde* (122); Angus Folk Museum, *Tayside* (122); Castle Ward, *Co. Down* (125); Springhill, *Co. Londonderry* (125).

17 *Out Shopping . . .* (page 38)

The Old Post Office at Tintagel is on the N coast of *Cornwall* in the centre of the village on B3263.

Winster is in *Derbyshire*. The Market House is in the village main street, on S side of B5057, 6 km (4 miles) W of Matlock.

Paycocke's is in *Essex*, in the village of Coggeshall on the S side of West Street (A120), 9 km (5½ miles) E of Braintree.

Gladstone's Land is in Edinburgh, *Lothian*, on the N side of the Lawnmarket.

Other old shops or displays include Chipping Campden Market Hall, *Gloucestershire* (109); Shugborough, *Staffordshire* (113); Lavenham Guildhall, *Suffolk* (115); Angus Folk Museum, *Tayside* (123); Gray's Printing Press, *Co. Tyrone* (125).

18 *Sit Still!* (page 40)

Sudbury Hall is in *Derbyshire*, 10 km (6 miles) E of Uttoxeter on A50.

Other schoolrooms or displays include Cragside, Wallington, *Northumberland* (119); Shugborough, *Staffordshire* (113); Angus Folk Museum, *Tayside* (123).

19 *Windpower* (page 42)

Pitstone Windmill is in *Buckinghamshire*, 0.8 km (½ mile) S of Ivinghoe, 5 km (3 miles) NE of Tring, just off B488.

Other windmills or wind devices can be found at Wicken Fen, *Cambridgeshire* (115); Lundy Island, *Devon* (99); Bembridge, *Isle of Wight* (105); Burnham Overy, Horsey, *Norfolk* (115); Lindisfarne, *Northumberland* (119); High Ham, *Somerset* (99).

20 *The Wellbrook Beetling Mill* (page 44)

Wellbrook is in *Co. Tyrone*, 5 km (3 miles) W of Cookstown on the Omagh road A505.

Other water-powered mills include Lode, *Cambridgeshire* (115); Nether Alderley, Quarry Bank, *Cheshire* (113); Cotehele, *Cornwall* (99); Bateman's, *East Sussex*, (105); Bourne, *Essex* (115); Dunham Massey, *Greater Manchester* (117); Dunster, *Somerset*, (100); Shalford, *Surrey* (105); Preston Mill, *Lothian* (123); Castle Ward, *Co. Down* (125).

21 *Beauty and the Beast* (page 46)

Aberdulais Falls are in *West Glamorgan* on A463, 5 km (3 miles) NW of Neath. O.S. Map 170: 772995.

Other ruins or remains of industrial sites include Dolaucothi, *Dyfed* (109); Beadnell Lime Kilns, *Northumberland* (119); Ravenscar Brickyards, *North Yorkshire* (120); Carding Mill, *Shropshire* (109); Hebden Dale, *West Yorkshire* (120).

22 *Restoring Styal* (page 48)

Styal village and mill are in *Cheshire*, 0.8 km ($\frac{1}{2}$ mile) NW of Wilmslow.

Other villages, or parts of villages, that have been restored by the Trusts include Blaise Hamlet, *Avon* (109); Boscastle harbour, *Cornwall* (100); Culross, *Fife* (123); Dunkeld, *Tayside* (123).

23 *Preserving Lacock* (page 50)

Lacock is in *Wiltshire*, 5 km (3 miles) S of Chippenham, just E of A350.

Other preserved villages, or parts of them, include West Wycombe, *Buckinghamshire* (110); Bohetherick, Bohortha, *Cornwall* (100); Branscombe, *Devon* (100); Chiddingstone, *Kent* (105); Coleshill, *Oxfordshire* (110); Hardwick, *Nottinghamshire* (113); Low Newton-by-the-Sea, *Northumberland* (120); Anstruther, Crail, Pittenweem, St Monans, *Fife* (123); Cushendun, *Co. Antrim* (125); Kearney, *Co. Down* (125).

24 *Cornish Engines* (page 52)

The East Pool and Agar Mine is in Camborne, *Cornwall*, on both sides of the A3047.

Other engine houses include Wheal Coates, Wheal Prosper, *Cornwall* (100); Wheal Betsy, *Devon* (100).

25 *Out for a Drink* (page 54)

The Tyn-y-Groes Hotel is in *Gwynedd*, 8 km (5 miles) NW of Dolgellau, on W side of A470.

The Fleece Inn is in *Hereford and Worcester* in the village of Bretforton, 6 km (4 miles) E of Evesham.

The Bachelors' Club is in *Strathclyde*, on B744 at Tarbolton, 12 km (8 miles) NE of Ayr off A758.

The Crown Liquor Saloon is in Great Victoria Street (opposite the Europa Hotel), *Belfast*.

Other pubs preserved by the Trust include the Cross Keys, the Tower Bank Arms, *Cumbria* (117); the Castle Inn, *East Sussex* (105); Spread Eagle, *Wiltshire* (105).

26 *Places of Worship* (page 56)

Tŷ Mawr is in *Gwynedd*, in the Wybrnant valley 6 km (3½ miles) SW of Betws-y-Coed. O.S. Map 115: 770524.

Sandham Memorial Chapel is in *Hampshire*, 6 km (4 miles) S of Newbury, just N of Burghclere, E of A34.

Iona is off the SW tip of Mull, *Strathclyde*; ferry from Oban to Craigmure, single road to Fionnphort and ferry.

Mussenden Temple is in *Co. Londonderry* at Downhill, 8 km (5 miles) W of Coleraine on A2.

Other places of worship include Keld, *Cumbria* (117); Loughwood, *Devon* (101); Staunton Harold, *Leicestershire* (114); Clumber, *Nottinghamshire* (114); Gibside, *Tyne and Wear* (120); Falkland Palace, *Fife* (123).

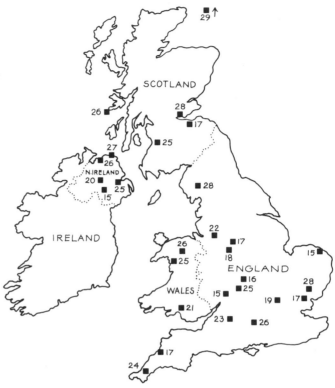

27 *The Fishermen of Carrick-a-rede* (page 58)

The Rope Bridge is in *Co. Antrim*, 8 km (5 miles) W of Ballycastle on the N Antrim coast.

Other special skills can be seen at the Boarstall Duck Decoy, *Buckinghamshire* (110).

28 *New Uses for Old Buildings* (page 60)

Bridge House is in *Cumbria* in the centre of Ambleside.

Lavenham Guildhall is in *Suffolk* in the market square.

Culross is in *Fife*, 19 km (12 miles) W of the Forth Road Bridge, off A985 via Torryburn.

Other old buildings with new uses can be found at Houghton Mill, *Cambridgeshire* (115); Bedruthan, *Cornwall* (101); Wembury Bay, *Devon* (101); Stonebarrow Hill, *Dorset* (101); Stackpole, *Dyfed* (109); Winchester City Mill, *Hampshire* (105); Blewcoat School, *London* (111); St George's Hall, *Norfolk* (116); Castle Ward, *Co. Down* (125).

29 *Fair Isle* (page 62)

Fair Isle is midway between Orkney and Shetland off the NE coast of *Scotland*; by air from Tingwall, Shetland, or by *The Good Shepherd* from Grutness, Shetland. Fair Isle is unique.

Marks Upon the Land

My introduction to the countryside was from the safety of my father's shoulders high above sly stinging nettles, spiky thistles and buzzing cowpats. As I grew older, my eyes looked further to fields and mountains. Streams became dam sites; rocks were castles to defend and trees were for climbing.

Only slowly did it dawn on me that much of this free, beautiful countryside had been shaped and marked by human beings. Trees had often been planted for a reason – as a future supply of timber, or to protect a building from gales. A rocky area might be the result of mining. The edge of a hillside field was determined not so much by Nature, but by the angle of steepness at which it was possible for a man and a horse to plough.

There are also oddities where people have made their own particular mark on the land. These landmarks are often on tops of hills for all to see, and one of Britain's oldest is the White Horse of Uffington. It was popular as long ago as the 12th century when it was known as one of the "Wonders of Britain". Archaeologists think it may even date from 500 BC but they are uncertain about its true date and purpose.

A more recent landmark is Paxton's Tower. In the 1802 General Election, the Conservatives asked a London banker, Sir William Paxton, to contest the Carmarthen county seat in South Wales. He promised the local people that if they elected him he would build them a bridge across the nearby River Towy, and during the fierce

Above: *Paxton's Tower dominates the skyline near the River Towy as much today as it did when it was built in 1811. It is known locally as Tŵr Spite.*

Below: *The White Horse of Uffington is one of England's oldest landmarks. Today it is threatened by too many feet.*

Right: *Mow Cop Castle, built by Randle Wilbraham in 1750, sits on top of a 335-metre escarpment. From Wilbraham's nearby home at Rode Hall, it looked the "perfect" castle for those who did not know any better!*

Below: The Hermitage, a folly built in 1758 near Dunkeld in Scotland. Wordsworth described it as a sick man's dream – he preferred the natural *beauty of the place. The round walls magnify the sound of the water, and in a flood it is a frightening spot.*

campaign he entertained his "supporters" on a truly lavish scale. He gave 11,070 breakfasts, 36,901 lunches, 684 suppers, 115,000 litres of beer, 11,068 bottles of whisky, 8,879 bottles of port, 460 bottles of sherry and 509 bottles of cider. The cost came to £15,690 4s 2d which included £786 on party election ribbons. When the great day came, Sir William *lost* by 117 votes. He was so furious that he built the tower overlooking the Towy valley as a reminder to the local people of his wealth and what they had missed.

Rich individuals like Paxton have left their marks in many ways. For example, Randle Wilbraham built himself a mock castle on top of a hill so that he had an eye-catching view from his house: but perhaps one of the best follies of all is the Hermitage. Perched overlooking a waterfall this little building used to have mirrors around the walls and ceiling so that it felt as if water was pouring in at you from all directions. Such were some of the marks of Man upon the land in the 18th century!

Modern landmarks

Whether you are walking to a hilltop site or playing hide and seek in a wood, or just enjoying a view, you are never far from the influence of human beings however natural you may think your surroundings are.

Today, *our* modern marks upon the land include motorways, industrial estates, electricity pylons and telecommunications towers spread across the length and breadth of Britain. Almost 100 years ago, the founders of the National Trust realised that the future of the countryside was becoming important – not just to farmers, but to the increasing numbers of city dwellers wanting to "escape" to the country. The threat which they foresaw in 1895 has developed into what is called "urbanisation". The spread of towns and cities is growing and as a result, we are losing about 50,000 acres of countryside every year (that is about 78 square miles).

The pressures that *all of us* are now putting upon our land are so great that if our countryside survives at all, it will be because people now and in the past have looked to the future and have decided to take action.

A Nibbled Landscape

One of the first beautiful areas of Britain to be threatened by development, and especially tourism, was the Lake District. Today, much of this popular holiday area, so near to the vast industrial cities of Lancashire and Yorkshire, is owned and protected by the National Trust.

This is because thousands of people over the years have given land, or collected money for the Trust to buy land, and so protect it for ever. The first collections and campaigns were led by two people. One was the fiery Hardwicke Rawnsley, a founder of the National Trust, and the other was a shy but determined woman.

Mrs Heelis of Sawrey

Mrs Heelis had known and admired Hardwicke Rawnsley since the 1870s when as a young girl she visited the Lake District with her parents on holidays. He encouraged her talent for drawing animals and, in 1901, helped her to publish a small children's book. She had so caught his infectious enthusiasm for the Lake District that in 1905 she bought a small farm in Sawrey with the profits from her successful book. By the time she married at the age of 47 in 1913, she had written several more children's books which earned her enough money to buy more farms.

Her greatest worry was the disappearance of Herdwick sheep from the upland slopes. She realised that without the sheep the high rolling grass hills would become covered by thistles, bushes and gorse. The sheep kept this growth under control by nibbling the young juicy shoots.

Below: *Mrs Heelis and her shepherd, Tom Storey, at a Lake District sheep fair. Mrs Heelis greatly admired the Herdwick breed. The colour of their fleece helps them absorb the sun's rays in the winter. Some sheep trapped under snow drifts have survived for up to a month by sucking the grease from the fleece on their backs.*

Herdwick sheep and the upland farms

Over hundreds of years, Herdwicks have evolved a perfect body for the high fells of the Lake District. Their strong bones support a short, stocky body which makes them nimble jumpers on the steep, rocky slopes. Best of all, the sheep do not need to be fenced in because they always stay within a few acres of the fell where they were born.

Despite these qualities, Herdwicks were quickly disappearing from the high fells during the early 1900s. Their rough fleece had been used to make cheap carpeting, which was being replaced by linoleum floor covering. Farmers began deserting their upland fells, introduced other breeds of sheep on to their lower pastures and supplemented their incomes from tourists who were discovering the beauty of the Lake District. What they failed to realise was that the beauty which the tourists admired was a result of the farmers keeping nibbling Herdwicks on the fells. Mrs Heelis decided to act.

She bought upland farms and reared Herdwick sheep *herself*. She could be seen at all the major sheep fairs, usually wearing wooden clogs and an old hat and coat, and with the help of her shepherds, she won many prizes for her tups, or rams. The money from her books allowed her to buy and save 14 upland farms and 4,000 acres (1,620 hectares) of nibbled fell which she left to the Trust.

Hardwicke Rawnsley would have been proud of the young girl he had encouraged. Her first children's story about a rabbit called Peter had led to other tales about Squirrel Nutkin, Mrs Tiggy-Winkle and Jeremy Fisher. Their success allowed Beatrix Potter (for that is who Mrs Heelis was) to buy and save farms for the future: working farms which otherwise would have been converted into holiday homes and whose high fells would now be covered with thistles, bushes and gorse.

Left: *The mountains of the Lake District were once wooded to their summits. It has taken between 4,000 and 5,000 years for Man's clearance of the woods, and nibbling sheep, to form the treeless fells that are so loved today.*

Above: *The coarse, grey wool which lost its market in the 1900s is being promoted by the National Trust today. Herdwick lambs are born black, but gradually turn grey as they become older. This results in an attractive grey-black wool.*

Right: *An injected Herdwick lamb is reunited with its mother. This upland farm was one of the first to be saved by Mrs Heelis and its high fells continue to be nibbled by Herdwick sheep.*

For Peat's Sake

Wicken Fen sits like the top of a giant rice pudding in the middle of Cambridgeshire surrounded by some of the best agricultural farmland in the British Isles. It is composed of a 6-metre layer of peat, the result of 3,000 years' accumulation of dead plants. The ground is so full of water that there is not enough oxygen to allow bacteria to decompose fully, or "eat", the dead vegetation and so it half rots to form peat.

The watery ground quivers and shakes when you walk on it and for much of the year a heavy tractor would break through the thin, drier "skin" on the surface and sink without trace. The soggy peat encourages the rapid growth of sedge and many wild flowering plants with tempting names like ragged robin, yellow rattle, comfrey and yellow loosestrife.

The Fen is also one of the few places in Britain where you can find non-stinging nettles, perhaps because no animals have ever been grazed on the Fen and so a sting has not been necessary.

Right: Wicken Fen has never been touched by farmers but it has been worked by Man for 1,000 years. Peat is dug, dried and burned as a fuel and sedge, a grasslike plant, is grown as thatching material. The Fen is rich in insect and bird life. Look for the bird hide on the skyline.

Buzz, flutter and crawl

Below: Bladderwort is found in stillwater ponds at Wicken Fen. It is a plant with small bags, or bladders, which are used to trap and digest tiny water creatures which accidentally touch the sensitive hairs around the bladder cap. The rush of water carries the creature inside.

The variety of plants and vegetation which has been cut continually by men for hundreds of years has led to the presence of over 5,000 species of insects on the Fen. These include brightly coloured beetles; damsel flies; hovering dragonflies; night-flying moths and day-fluttering butterflies. This rich insect life attracted entomologists to Wicken in the last century. They recorded insects which they caught and built private collections of butterflies, moths and beetles. But towards the end of the century, local farmers wanted to drain the Fen and use the rich land for growing crops. The entomologists opposed this by buying small plots of the Fen which they began giving to the Trust in 1899 so that Wicken Fen would remain a nature reserve for ever.

When the peat runs out

East Anglia is Britain's most important food-growing area. The farmers have drained most of the Fens and can grow crops easily on the flat, rich peat. But there is a problem. When peat is drained, the top layer dries to dust which strong winds blow away.

The 6-metre layer of peat is wasting away – and it cannot be replaced. In some places the "wastage" has been as much as 4 metres in just ten years. Even coffins in peat graveyards have been exposed. The average wastage rate is now estimated at 2.5 cm a year. In some places the peat will have disappeared by the year AD 2000. Some farmers are so concerned about the loss of peat on their land that they are draining away less water to conserve their precious supplies of peat. In the future, they may well turn for advice to Wicken Fen – one of the few places which still retains its layer of peat.

Right: *Some parts of the Fen are left to provide tree cover for birds and wildlife. Here a line of fencing stakes has grown into a line of willow trees because of the richness of the ground!*

Below left: *A wind pump that once drained the land now pumps water back into the Fen to retain the peat supply.*

Below right: *The sedge is cut and stacked and then sold as thatching material for roofs.*

The Man who gave away Mountains

Unlike Mrs Heelis in the Lake District and the entomologists of Wicken Fen who were concerned with "man-made" landscapes, Percy Unna was a wealthy Englishman who wanted to save wild parts of Scotland. A civil engineer by trade, he was also a keen mountaineer who loved walking and climbing in raw, wild unmarked countryside. His love of this scenery was so strong that he bought mountains so that they would always remain wild.

Above: *The wildness of Glen Coe which appealed so much to Percy Unna remains its greatest attraction to mountaineers today.*

The Unna guidelines of 1937

Unna, with help from mountaineering clubs, gave the mountains to the National Trust for Scotland with certain recommendations:
- the mountains should *not* be made easier or safer to climb
- old paths should *not* be repaired nor new paths made
- *no* roads or tracks should be built in the mountains
- there should be *no* signposts, paint marks or heaps of stones, called cairns, to help people find their way
- *no* shelters or café huts should be built on the mountains.

In short, Unna wanted to keep the mountains wild and dangerous so that walking in them remained a difficult challenge. This meant that the only people who could walk in these remote places were people fit enough to carry their own supplies and who knew the mountains so well that there was little risk of getting lost.

72

The pressures of today

Unna's guidelines have become difficult to follow because more people have cars, holidays are longer and we assume that we can "park and walk" just about anywhere we like.

Unfortunately too many people come unprepared for sudden and dramatic changes in weather that can turn streams into torrents or a view over a dizzy precipice into a blank wall of cold, grey cloud. There have been more accidents; more people have died on the mountains; and more paths have become dangerously eroded by thousands of feet. The Trust decided they could no longer do nothing, and in two popular places, Glen Coe and Ben Lawers, they give advice and information from visitor centres.

This has angered some mountaineers who say that the wild mountains should be left alone; that wildness *is* dangerous, and that the last, few unmarked places must *never* be made easier to find or explore.

The future of these places needs to be discussed because our power today is truly great. We can, for example:

- build cable cars to the tops of mountains and lift ourselves into "instant wildness"
- choose to do nothing and leave the mountains free for a small number of fit climbers who have the time and ability to reach the wildness they value so much
- educate more people about the mountains in a way that tries to preserve their wildness but which allows more people to experience and therefore respect it.

The choice is ours – the future is our children's.

Below: *The Ben Lawers boardwalk provides a single route across a sensitive area. The visitor centre in the background gives advice and information to people who want to explore the mountains.*

A Day in the Life of a Warden

The Carneddau range is in a mountainous region of North Wales used by climbers, campers, farmers, day-trippers and many other groups of people. Simon Lapington is the National Trust Warden of this popular place and these are just some of the jobs he does to preserve the wildness of the Carneddau while at the same time allowing people to experience them both now and in the future.

Morning

Breakfast and post. Coffee and toast. An army letter confirms that the Royal Engineers will build a bridge for us over one of the streams while they are here on exercise. There's a letter from a school. Could I give a talk on the Carneddau to their 2nd and 3rd years, please? Another letter. The mountain rescue services want to do a night exercise next week and could they use our bunkhouse as a base? I must check that the local farmer won't mind them using tracker dogs.

After breakfast, I drive 6 miles (10 km) to pick up a secondhand cooker someone has kindly donated to the bunkhouse. We get volunteer groups all year who do conservation work for us in return for free accommodation.

On the way back I stop to see a farmer. He's got a problem. Visitors have been picking up lambs and returning them to his farm because they think the lambs are lost. Could I make some signs (especially before the Bank Holiday) asking people to leave the lambs alone. Oh, and could I keep reminding dog owners about dogs and leads, please. *Diolch yn fawr* – thank you.

Further down the valley I finish planting a small shelter belt of young bushes. In five years' time they will provide an extra supply of insects for the growing numbers of pipits, wheatears and chats which are nesting nearby.

I check out a previous army-built bridge on my way to a coffee at Dennis's cafe. He's the ears and eyes of the valley and always knows what is going on. No reports of motorbike scramblers today, but some climbers reported a small landslip on one of the paths above the lake. By the way, had I seen the abandoned Cortina on one of the campsites?

On to another farm where I finish putting protective wire around young ash trees planted last week. In about fifteen years' time, they will provide extra shelter for the farmhouse. Two ladies are exercising their dogs. Oh yes, they're very good with sheep. Yes, they *will* keep them on leads. Back home for lunch.

Afternoon

Lunch and the phone and some time on my own. Could the police check out an abandoned Cortina, please?

It's fine for the army to land a helicopter tomorrow, but could they land on Dafydd Williams' field as the other farmer has been having lambing problems.

When is the timber arriving for repairs to one of the barns? I confirm we want to keep the old slates as I'm sure we'll want to use them one of these days. No, stack them in the yard.

Hello, it's Simon Lapington from the National Trust. Could you *please* deliver the underground telephone cable this week. Yes, we've finished the trench and we're waiting for the cable.

After lunch, I spot a film crew making a television commercial. Did they realise they were on Trust property? Have you had permission to film here? Yes, I know it's very beautiful, but it all costs money to keep it that way. No, I'm sorry, you can't go on filming until you have paid a fee. Now look, you couldn't make scenery like this in a studio, could you? It must be worth something or you wouldn't be here.

Visit to a volunteer group digging drainage ditches beside a path. Could two of you go back to the bunkhouse, please, and make four signs saying, "Please do not approach or handle new born lambs." Thanks. Can I have four volunteers? There's been a landslip higher up. No, don't bring any tools – we'll use the picks and shovels which are hidden up there.

On the way up, we stop and look through binoculars at a small group of wild goats way up the mountain. I just keep a quiet eye on them as they look after themselves pretty well.

By the way, you see that little island over there? The sheep can't reach and nibble it, and it shows what the area would look like if there weren't any nibbling sheep to keep the bushes and heather under control. Every few years a dollop of heather on the rock falls into the water because it has grown too big. Right, lesson over. Let's get to the landslip!

Three hours later, it's back home for a bath. Telephone rings. It's a farmer who is furious because a couple of dogs have been chasing his sheep. It has made him think twice about allowing visitors to wander freely on his land, especially as they've been using his stone wall as ammunition in a stream.

I'll go and make some repairs on Saturday and keep my eyes skinned for loose dogs. Most people are sensible, but there's always one or two ... could I chat to him tomorrow about a mountain rescue exercise next week? *Diolch yn fawr.*

Supper. Telephone rings. It's a writer doing a book on the Trust. Could he spend a day with me next month to get an idea of the sort of job I do. In a day? He'll be lucky!

A Mystery to Unearth

Underneath the fields around Avebury in Wiltshire, there lies a secret which one day somebody might unearth. It is a 4,000-year-old mystery which attracts over 200,000 visitors a year. It is a gigantic puzzle of at least 180 stones weighing between 15 and 45 tonnes *each*, up to 3 metres high and arranged in three circles – two small ones within a larger circle.

The whole area is surrounded by an enormous, circular ditch 1,350 metres long and 9 metres deep. The 150 *thousand* tonnes of chalk which were dug by hand out of the ditch were used to build an outer bank which is 5 metres high. So why did people nearly 4,000 years ago go to so much trouble to build this extraordinary place?

We simply do not know.

Destruction

In fact, we are lucky to be able to see the 37 stones which now stand at Avebury because people have been pulling them down or smashing them up for hundreds of years.

In the 7th century, some of the stones were used to build a church. Later, during the 1300s, many stones were buried because people thought that they were evil. During the 18th century, more stones were smashed and used in buildings in Avebury village. Other stones were broken up and cleared away so that the land could be farmed and, later, even more were shattered and used as road foundations.

Top left: *Avebury village encircled by its mysterious stones and huge earth bank.*

Above: *In 1938, Alexander Keiller set up a museum in the coach house and stable of Avebury Manor so that visitors could see his discoveries and learn more about the stones and other nearby prehistoric sites.*

For example, at Windmill Hill the skeleton of a young child was excavated from ditch number 111. It dates from 3160 BC and now lies in a special floor case in the museum.

Above: *Stone number nine (far right in photograph) was re-erected by Keiller and his helpers. You can see how big it is in the photograph above which shows all the block and tackle needed to lift the heavy weight.*

The stone had been buried in the 14th century, and when Keiller raised it he found a skeleton of a barber-surgeon (below). *From that day on, the stone has been known as the Barber Stone.*

A skeleton is found

In 1934, an archaeologist called Alexander Keiller bought the stones and much of Avebury village to stop any further destruction. To the villagers' surprise, he began marking the positions of the missing stones and started to re-erect the fallen or buried ones.

Underneath one massive stone, Keiller and his helpers found a skeleton of a man and next to it the remains of a leather purse which contained coins dated 1300 and 1307. This confirmed that the unfortunate man had died during one of the 14th-century burials of the stones. Presumably the great stone had toppled on him while they were digging earth from underneath it and no doubt his ghastly death, writhed out to screams of pain, added to the myth that the stones were evil.

Preservation for the future

For the moment, little archaeological excavation is done inside the circle and more time is spent preserving the stones and the earthworks from damage by the thousands of visitors every year. Instead, the archaeologists are waiting for a time when they will have more sophisticated ways of "seeing" underground without disturbing or uncovering the soil. Already some of the technology used in finding oil in the North Sea is of interest and computers, lasers and sonar equipment might one day help to explain some of Avebury's secrets.

At present we can only guess the purpose of the stones. Were they used as some kind of religious temple or were they part of a giant mathematical calculator? Could they have been used to plot the movements of planets or were they a ceremonial site which was linked to the growing of crops?

Whatever our guesses, Avebury now waits – protected and safe – for the future to unearth its mysterious past.

The Wey Ahead

The River Wey meanders through meadows and slips along Surrey back gardens. The 20-mile section from Godalming to Weybridge was first opened to boats over 200 years ago after locks and control gates had been built to regulate the flow of water and to raise and lower boats at natural waterfalls.

The navigators, or navvies, straightened the sharpest bends in the river, widened some narrow stretches and dug artificial channels along other sections near the river.

Timber and corn were carried by barge along the Wey for nearly 200 years but when the railway opened in 1845, barge traffic began to decline.

In the 1960s the river from Godalming to Weybridge was given to the Trust by its owners in order to preserve the Wey as a peaceful place for leisure activities. Today, cruising barges can be hired for holidays afloat. A few people live permanently on the river in houseboats. Others use the river for fishing, canoeing or birdwatching, while the towpaths provide good walks or painting viewpoints.

On a warm summer's day all is peaceful and calm. The river idly floats by on its way to the Thames and the North Sea; couples walk hand in hand along the towpath; boats chug to and fro; children play hide and seek; families finish their picnics; bees hum; birds chirp; all is peaceful.

The river simply looks after itself – or so it seems.

Volunteer party clears supermarket trollies and rubbish from canal section. Move upstream 3 squares – Bonus

Gates smashed by careless boatman but repairs completed just before busy Bank Holiday

Boat stuck on storm weir needs to be towed off

River drained and sewage pipes laid well before start of the boating season

Cattle trample section of bank which needs rebuilding

Fallen tree needs clearing

Painting of bridge finished

Good dredging progress

Stiles repaired and all access paths cleared

START

Downstream

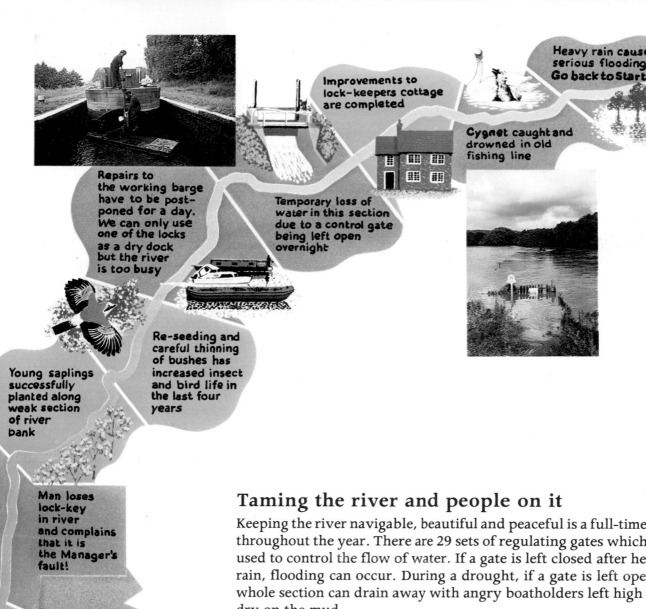

Heavy rain causes serious flooding. Go back to Start!

FINISH

Improvements to lock-keepers cottage are completed

Cygnet caught and drowned in old fishing line

Repairs to the working barge have to be postponed for a day. We can only use one of the locks as a dry dock but the river is too busy

Temporary loss of water in this section due to a control gate being left open overnight

Re-seeding and careful thinning of bushes has increased insect and bird life in the last four years

Young saplings successfully planted along weak section of river bank

Man loses lock-key in river and complains that it is the Manager's fault!

GUILDFORD

How to play "Weyplay" – an exciting new game that tests your patience at managing the River Wey.

Start downstream on the bottom left square. Throw a dice for each move. Green squares are safe. Move downstream two places on all red squares. The winner is the first to reach the upstream finish.

Taming the river and people on it

Keeping the river navigable, beautiful and peaceful is a full-time job throughout the year. There are 29 sets of regulating gates which are used to control the flow of water. If a gate is left closed after heavy rain, flooding can occur. During a drought, if a gate is left open, a whole section can drain away with angry boatholders left high and dry on the mud.

Old trees with dangerous overhanging branches have to be felled, while young saplings are planted to provide shelter and to hold the banks firm with their root systems.

There are towpaths, bridges, signs, stiles and lock keepers' cottages to look after. The access footpaths, which allow people to get to the river, have to be maintained – stinging nettles need cutting and brambles have to be controlled. In some places the river may need to be dredged.

The biggest problem of all is from people ramming into lock gates by mistake, or driving boats too fast and causing a wash that erodes the delicate earth banks. All the repairs cost money, which comes mostly from licences and mooring charges.

Looking to the future

Despite all the problems, the River Wey is steadily improving because of its constant use and continual repairs. Over the years, the locks have been rebuilt, lock gates have been renewed and better water sealants are preventing leakages. By using the river sensibly, the navigation is gradually improving, and it looks to the future with confidence. It also provides fun and pleasure to the thousands of people who use it in so many different ways.

Save our Coast!

A wild, unpredictable sea surrounds the British Isles and childhood memories of it, like the tides, never ebb away completely. They flow back as rippling waves on a calm day creep their way over hot, summer sand.

Pools exposed at low tide flicker and dart with glimpses of life from another world. Steep cliffs tempt you to fly, and turn your stomach at the thought.

Hide and seek dunes; pebbly, barefoot hobbles to a weightbearing sea; sandwiches covered in sand; castles braving the tide; surf, spray and "away for the day!" There is so much more to the sea than just sea.

And yet, in the 1960s, about 6 miles (9 km) of unspoilt coastline a year were being lost to industrial development, sprawling holiday resorts and creeping caravan parks.

A survey at the time showed that of the 3,000 miles (4,800 km) of coast round Britain, approximately one third had been ruined for ever. Another third was neither beautiful nor particularly important. But the remaining 980 miles (1,568 km) *were* of great beauty and importance and were under threat.

The Enterprise Neptune campaign

Although the Trust already protected 187 miles (300 km) of coastline, it launched a campaign in 1965 to raise £2 million in order to buy and save beautiful stretches of coast for ever. Donations from children, pensioners, landowners and businessmen added up to £1 million by August 1967 and by June the following year a further 100 miles (160 km) had been saved. In October 1973, another £1 million saved another 100 miles.

By 1982, a total of over £5½ million of donations had saved 430 miles (668). There remains a final 500 miles (800 km) of beautiful coast at risk and Enterprise Neptune continues.

Above and below: *The steps at Bedruthan wind down to a beautiful rock and sand beach. The time is 10 am.*

Above and left: *By 7 pm on the same day Bedruthan beach looks very different.*

That is part of the fascination and importance of our everchanging coastline.

Building and destroying

Above and below: Seagulls soar round the cliffs near Ballintoy in Northern Ireland.

On the far headland there used to be a lime and basalt quarry with ugly towers which dominated the beautiful bay. In 1979, the Trust blew them up.

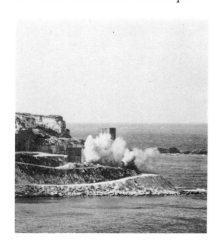

The ever-changing sea destroys cliffs and headlands but builds beaches and sand dunes. The coastline is forever changing and the photographs on these pages show the Trust's response to two very different places which were bought with Enterprise Neptune money.

The first is the breathtakingly steep staircase at Bedruthan in north Cornwall. The dizzy steps plunge their way to the beach below. Over the years, the bottom steps had been washed away and it was impossible to reach the beautiful beach. But in 1974, the Trust rebuilt them so that once again there was a way down to this exciting but dangerous place.

The second example concerns a wide sweep of part of the coast near Ballintoy in Northern Ireland. There used to be a lime and basalt quarry right on the tip of the headland with ugly buildings and towers which were visible from the whole bay. In 1978, the Trust bought the old, disused quarry and on Thursday, 27 September 1979, the army was ready to blow up the buildings.

The villagers of Ballintoy gathered to watch. A rocket signal was fired. The charges exploded. When the dust settled, the towers were still standing, so a second attempt was made three days later. This time it worked!

A car park is being built out of sight in the heart of the old quarry and eventually a footpath will lead from it to the famous rope bridge at Carrick-a-Rede which swings nearby.

81

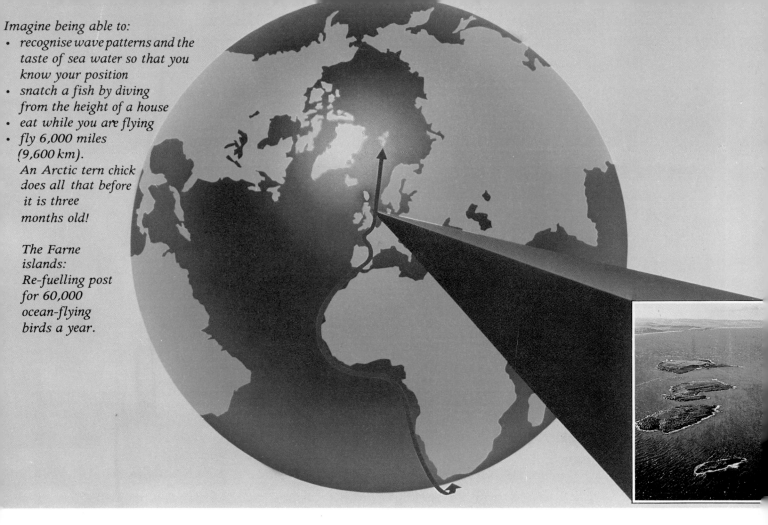

Imagine being able to:
- recognise wave patterns and the taste of sea water so that you know your position
- snatch a fish by diving from the height of a house
- eat while you are flying
- fly 6,000 miles (9,600 km).
  An Arctic tern chick does all that before it is three months old!

The Farne islands: Re-fuelling post for 60,000 ocean-flying birds a year.

On the Wing

The Farnes are a group of 20 small islands lying about 3 miles (5 km) off the Northumberland coast near good supplies of fish. Every year 60,000 sea birds of 17 different species use the islands. Some of them stay all the year round, while others come to breed in late spring. There are also winter visitors and migrants who stop to refuel on their journeys which cover distances of about 10,000 miles (16,000 km).

The islands are especially busy in spring when thousands of birds collect seaweed and grass to build their nests. Later their mates are busy catching food for their young. Catching live fish is difficult because the water refracts the light and magnifies the fish which makes them seem closer and bigger than they really are.

Defence

Each species of bird has its own defence system. Guillemots and cormorants nest together in great numbers for protection. Kittiwakes nest near fierce-looking shags which have bright eyes and a yellow streak down the side of their beaks. Fulmars give out a foul-smelling fluid from their nostrils. Eider ducks camouflage themselves among the sea campions.

But the birds cannot protect themselves from poachers' traps or coastal developments, which is why, in 1925, bird enthusiasts collected money to buy the Farnes as a permanent sanctuary.

Below: *There is safety in numbers for these nesting guillemots and cormorants. The guillemots lay pear-shaped eggs which roll in a circle and so do not fall off ledges.*

82

Above: *An Arctic tern on the wing.*

Migration

The Arctic tern is surely the most spectacular traveller around the world because it flies from the Arctic to the Antarctic *and back* every year of its adult life. That can add up to total of over 500,000 miles (800,000 km).

Bird experts think that the terns find their way by using the sun, stars and a sort of magnetic compass in their heads. Ornithologists also think that the birds know when to leave the Farnes by linking the daytime temperature to the actual length of day, but no-one is sure how they do it.

Ringing for information

In order to find out more about the birds and their lives at sea, wardens on the Farnes put numbered rings around the legs of as many as 7,000 birds a year and keep exact records of the numbers and species which use the islands.

The wardens also grow and replant the sea campions which provide Eiders and Puffins with camouflage and shelter, but which are ruined by seals who roll and slide on them!

Careful management of the islands has increased the numbers of visiting birds from 40,000 to 60,000 a year since 1971. Over 30,000 people a year visit the islands which are open from April until the end of September. School parties and holidaymakers follow special nature trails and marvel at the sight of so many birds living together.

Without sanctuaries like the Farnes, we would never be able to get near enough to study or film the birds as easily as we can. If we did not go out of our way to preserve a habitat for them, many species would become extinct and our cliffs and shores would echo to the sound of seagulls only.

The Farnes, and other nature reserves like them, give the busy migratory birds a chance to rest or breed in safety. They also give us a chance to find out more about their puzzling lives at sea and on the wing navigating their way around a hostile world.

Right: *Irresistible Puffins — these characters can hold a line of ten small fish in their bills. The fish usually lie alternately head to tail which suggests that the birds zig-zag their way through shoals of fish.*

A series of hooks on their "adjustable" beaks means that puffins can hold on to several fish while catching others at the same time.

We still do not know how the puffins return to the Farnes at the same time in late March.

Above: *Castle Ward tower. Is there anything odd about it?*

Left and below: *Look how big the stone pineapple really is! The urns on either side of the pineapple are chimneys.*

Look Again

There are many signposted oddities, follies and viewpoints around the British Isles that are always worth a second look. They make good spots for breaking journeys, or as an aim for a walk, or as somewhere to take a visitor. Here are four:

The Pineapple

The photograph *(above)* shows the superb stonework of "The Pineapple" near Stirling in Scotland. It was built in 1761 for the 29-year-old Earl of Dunmore who later became a Governor of New York and Virginia. Every stone "leaf" has drainage holes at the bottom so that they cannot be damaged by frost. This extraordinary summer house was given to the National Trust for Scotland and is leased to the Landmark Trust who restored it and who now rent it as a holiday pineapple. One affectionate entry in the logbook says, "Farewell old fruit."

The Castle Ward tower

Castle Ward in Northern Ireland has a defensive tower house in its farmyard. It was built in 1610 by Nicholas Ward. Not to be outdone, a later Ward added a clock to the old building in 1887. His name was William and he left his mark in an unusual way. Have a closer look at the top middle photograph.

Right: *Watlington church and its splendid spire of 1764.*

Right: *Watlington church and its splendid spire of 1764.*

Symbols which lead to treasure. (Top) The National Trust for Scotland and (above) the National Trust in the rest of the British Isles.

The Watlington Spire

In the 18th century a gentleman by the name of Edward Horne, Esquire, lived in the Oxfordshire village of Watlington. He travelled daily by carriage to Oxford and was comforted to see church spires all the way to work. However, the return journey disappointed him because Watlington church did not aspire to a spire. The Squire conspired to build a spire 82 metres long by 11 metres wide at its base. It was cut into the chalk hills behind the church and enabled Edward Horne to see spires along his *return* journey too!

The Dolaucothi mines

The Romans mined gold for their coins at Dolaucothi, Dyfed, and it is possible to enter the caves all year and some of the deeper mines in summer. There is a Roman aqueduct 7 miles (11 km) long which brought $13\frac{1}{2}$ million litres of water to the site every 24 hours. The mines are near Pumpsaint and are well worth a visit, as are all the outdoor sites which are marked by the two Trust symbols. So keep looking!

Right: *One of the Roman caves which was once mined for gold at Dolaucothi, 8 miles (13 km) south east of Lampeter off the A482 at Pumpsaint, Dyfed.*

85

In the Mind's Eye

The only living things on earth that are able to convert sunlight into energy are plants. We pride ourselves in suntans but plants store the sun's energy which we need to eat in order to remain alive.

Apart from food, plants also provide us with rubber, cotton and drugs and yet we have exploited only 4 per cent of the estimated 250,000 species of plants which grow in our world.

It comes as a bit of a shock, therefore, to realise that many of our most colourful plants, which we call flowers, are in fact made by man. Again and again we have used various features of a plant such as its smell, colour or height for our own purposes. Plant hunters have travelled all over the world in order to bring back species of plants which can be nurtured and cross-fertilised to suit our own needs. The skilful gardener who plants these seeds and flowers for us to enjoy is in fact growing live pictures which begin in his or her mind's eye.

Right: A trainee gardener plants out a border at Nymans Garden according to a plan. The date is 21 May.

Two months later, on 27 July, the result is still growing.

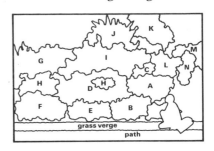

A summer border

In the top right photograph the head gardener has marked out lines and circles of sand and told the young trainee gardener *exactly* what to plant and where.

The box contains mallow "Mont Blanc" (a) which comes from the Mediterranean area. The seedlings were grown in a hothouse and are now ready for planting. The gardener knows that they will grow into a mass of white flowers which will help to show off the "Pink Apricot" antirrhinums (b) which are planted in front of the mallow, between the box and white post. Behind the mallow there is a clump of large-leaved canna (c) which grow in Central America. Each winter they are kept indoors. Their tall, straight, dark leaves will stand out behind the white mallow.

The dahlias (d), originally from Mexico, are also brought indoors each winter and will need bamboo canes to hold them up straight when they produce their large yellow flowers. Purple "Sugar Daddy" petunias (e) from South America will be planted in front of the dahlias. On their left are sweet-smelling tobacco plants (f) from Brazil. Hazel twigs will support a high-growing plant called golden rod (g) from the United States. Between this and the tobacco plants, the gardener wants red and white phlox (h) whose colours will blend and link the "Crimson Rock" tobacco plants, the red "Grüss An Teplitz" rose (i) and the mallow. Along the back of the border there are plants and bushes which remain all year. The buddleia (j), from China, attracts butterflies. On its right is a Japanese clerodendron (k). The white-leaved weigela (l) from Korea will have cream and green leaves in the summer. The wisteria (m) will not be visible in August but the clematis (n) with its deep purple flowers will punctuate the border like an exclamation mark. By then the gardener's picture will be ours too.

Below: Did you ever have a picture in your mind's eye of "Mary, Mary quite contrary's" garden? Here is someone's idea of it at Mount Stewart Garden in Northern Ireland.

Stone Cold

In the grounds of Shugborough, Staffordshire, there is a memorial dedicated to Admiral Anson's cat, which accompanied its master on a voyage round the world from 1740 to 1744. A stone cat sits on top of a large urn. The rectangular tablet on the main pedestal is artificial Coade stone which was made in the 18th century by Mrs Coade's extraordinary formula of clay, sand and secret ingredients. The stone is very tough, and when Mrs Coade died the secret formula died with her, and no-one has been able to copy it since.

More tragic stones lie on a cold hillside in Derbyshire near the village of Eyam. In the autumn of 1665, Eyam's tailor received a box of cloth from London which contained deadly plague-carrying fleas and within two days he had caught the ghastly disease. Panic gripped Eyam as the Plague spread. The first signs on a victim were swellings and a rosy-red rash of circles on the body. This was followed by high fever and sneezing which was how people thought the disease was spread. They carried posies of herbs and sniffed them in a vain attempt to disinfect their noses. But once anyone caught the Plague, it was almost certain that they would collapse and die. The brave villagers decided to stay within Eyam so as not to spread the disease further. They were left food at certain spots around the village. Within a year, 267 out of 350 of them were dead.

Seven graves mark the spot where one poor mother suffered terribly. On 3 August 1666 Mrs Hancock buried a son and daughter. On 7 August she buried her husband and two other sons. On 9 August she buried another daughter and on 10 August her last daughter, Ann – all alone with cold stone.

Above: *The Cat Monument.*

Below: *Most of the Hancock family are buried at Riley Graves, Eyam, Derbyshire.*
"Ring-a-ring of roses,
  A pocket full of posies.
  Atishoo, atishoo,
  We all fall down."

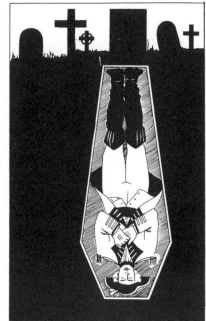

On the north west brow of Box Hill in Surrey there is a stone among the trees. Some believe that it marks the grave of an officer of the marines called Major Peter Labelliere, who, according to his wishes, was buried 30 metres down standing on his head.

Tradition has it that Labelliere believed that at the Resurrection and the end of the world, "everything would be turned topsy-turvy". And so the forward-planning Major reckoned that he at least would land on his feet.

More serious stones mark the spot where the last battle on British soil was fought in 1746.

Above: "... and there followed flashes of lightning and peals of thunder, and a violent earthquake, like none before it in human history, so violent it was. The great city was split in three: the cities of the world fell in ruin ..."
Revelation, *Chapter 16, vv. 18 and 19.*

Culloden Moor was where the Government troops of George II defeated the Jacobite army of Bonnie Prince Charlie. Within an hour there were more than 1,000 Jacobite dead and the loyalty of the troops who fought "in the wrong place on the wrong day" attracts many visitors to this day. The inscription on the memorial cairn put up in 1881 simply reads:

Below: The memorial cairn marks the area where the fiercest fighting of the Battle of Culloden took place.

THE BATTLE
OF CULLODEN
WAS FOUGHT ON THIS MOOR
16TH APRIL, 1746
THE GRAVES OF THE
GALLANT HIGHLANDERS
WHO FOUGHT FOR
SCOTLAND AND PRINCE CHARLIE
ARE MARKED BY THE NAMES
OF THEIR CLANS

Much of the battle area has been planted with fir trees but, with the co-operation of the Forestry Commission, the National Trust for Scotland will restore the landscape to its earlier moorland state. This will make it easier for visitors to appreciate what Culloden must have looked like in 1746.

Common Ground

In the days before freezers, supermarkets and Cellophane-wrapped portions of meat, people often kept a pig or a couple of chickens in their backyards. Bigger animals like horses, cows, sheep and donkeys were kept, or grazed, on special open areas called commons.

Witley Common, in Surrey, was used in this way for hundreds of years until the beginning of this century. At that time, cars began to replace horses, and refrigeration made it possible to move dead meat from one country to another. The need for people to have their own animals quickly disappeared, and without the grazing animals, commons began to change. Young, juicy seedlings of bushes and trees, which had always been eaten by the animals, began to grow larger. As they did so, they blocked out the sunlight and this in turn began to push out the heather and the bracken of the old Common. Slowly but steadily the open Common began to change into a closed wood.

Above: *Grazing cattle on the Common in 1906 painted by Sutton-Palmer.*

Two world wars

In 1914 and 1939, the growth of the trees on Witley Common was stopped dramatically by the building of army camps in World Wars I and II. The trees were cut down; concrete was laid; huts were built; and tanks carved deep tracks in the soft soil.

After World War II, all the huts were pulled down; the concrete was ripped up and loads of new soil, including chalk, were dumped to fill the trenches and gaps left by the camp. Once again the Common began to change.

The new soils meant that different grasses, wild flowers, shrubs and bushes began to grow and these in turn attracted different insects which attracted different birds. Within 20 years, Witley Common had become a most *un*common place.

Gently does it

You have to walk slowly and quietly through the Common today before you begin to notice things. There are sunny paths cut, not just for you, but also for butterflies that power their wings by sunlight. In some places hawthorn bushes have been cut in such a way that they provide thick cover for wrens, dunnocks and nightingales which only nest in thick, low bushes. There's a movement in a clump of willow trees. Something catches your eye. The clatter of wings as a wood pigeon lands on its nest high in the branches of a tall pine tree is followed by the "plop" of a dropping acorn. You look back at the willow trees and suddenly a roe deer turns her head and trots further into the wood.

Tap, tap . . . pause . . . tap. A woodpecker can be heard but not seen. As you walk into bright sunlight where the trees have been cut by man, a lizard darts into safe bracken. An adder sleeps drowsily on a sunny tuft of heather. The more you look, the more you see.

Below: *The Common as an army camp in World War II.*

The race for light:
One part of Witley Common has been left to Nature as an experiment. The birch trees in the background have been growing for about 40 years. Part of the old Common of bracken and heather is shown in the foreground.

There are evergreen Scots pines on the far left and the far right, and there is one tall silver birch on the right.

In the wood there is a race between the birch trees and some oak trees which are just beginning to appear above the birch. You can see them best in the middle summer photograph. As the oaks grow taller they will start to block out light needed by the birch trees. Fallen leaves will change the composition of the soil which will eventually favour the oaks rather than the birch. In summer, the bracken grows tall and young saplings in the foreground are growing quickly.

In the autumn, the warden and some young volunteer helpers control the unwanted sapling growth by pulling the young trees out of the ground. Some older Scots pines are also cut so that the old Common will remain a haven for wildlife that lives in heather and bracken.

Meanwhile the wood in the background is left untouched. It is a giant outdoors experiment and we think that the oak trees will take over the wood eventually. By the year AD 2040 it will certainly look different. If you were aged between nine and fourteen in 1980, you will be in your seventies by then, and with luck you might be able to take a look at the experiment that will never end!

Planning for Leisure

Planning in our countryside comes in many different shapes and sizes. From the trees of Witley Common to the bird cries on the Farnes, management is important and necessary in our hard-pressed land. Planning for our leisure includes the resiting of car parks *away* from beautiful stretches of coastline; planting trees to screen campsites; using local traditional materials in new buildings; repairing footpaths, bridges and steps; providing signposts and building wheelchair ramps.

Planning may also involve laying telephone wires underground or hiding an ugly electricity sub-station in an old, disused building. Even roadside verges have been bought by the Trusts to prevent a track becoming a widened road.

Refreshments and information centres are often necessary and benches for weary legs are always welcomed. All these things have to be thoughtfully planned.

Below: *Thousands of hands have polished this wooden post on a stile at a popular site.*

Is it really necessary?

The best answer is to look out for places where there is *no* planning or management. There are many examples around the country ranging from glinting windscreens on the tops of beautiful cliffs and hills to broken bottles around buzzing litter bins.

Thousands of booted feet can turn mossy paths into knobbly, stony, ankle-twisting assault courses that wear you out and force you to look where you tread.

Beautiful views are ruined by electricity pylons – mini Eiffel towers humming power from the generators to our homes.

How many times have you tried to reach a beach only to find that your way is blocked by lines of holiday bungalows or rows of caravans?

Look out for pink, concrete garages tacked on to old stone houses, or rusting corrugated farm buildings in the middle of a field, and signposts that remain vandalised for years. These are sure signs of non-planning and no management. The pressures that we are putting on our countryside are so great that one estimate claims we are losing green, open spaces at the rate of an area the size of Berkshire every *five* years.

So what should we do?

We must take the situation seriously and get involved ourselves because the problem is not going to simply "go away". Our beautiful outdoor places need to be visited, understood, looked after, paid for, enjoyed and, above all, shared. They belong to *all* of us and are deep in our Nation's roots.

If we rip them up, we will have only steel, concrete, glass, asphalt, brick and plastic to turn to for our wonder, beauty and peace.

The soft fields, colourful woods, marshes, moors, beaches and prattling streams rarely look after themselves. We have managed them in one way or another for centuries. Now we must protect and manage them for leisure purposes too in a way that does not spoil them. It is a delicate, difficult challenge.

An unusual example of sensitive planning is shown below. The sand dunes on this popular beach were in danger of literally being blown away by the wind and too many trampling feet. Natural hollows made good picnic spots but the more they were used, the less stable the dunes became. Instead of banning people from them, the wardens have designed human "nests" which they hope will hold the sand steady while at the same time allowing people to enjoy and use the beautiful dunes.

Left and below: *Two very different approaches. At popular sites like Bodiam Castle, cars and picnics are part of a day out, while on Lundy Island no cars are allowed.*

Considerable planning and imagination by the Landmark Trust has gone into the restoration of various buildings on Lundy. The lighthouse can be rented for a quiet holiday.

Right: *The dune "nests" at the Murlough Nature Reserve in Northern Ireland have proved to be popular with holiday makers who rush to "book their nest" early on summer mornings. The photograph shows the reserve in winter when the wardens hope that the dune grass will have a chance to grow around the nests, which will help to hold the sand and protect it from the wind.*

Getting Involved

The first way of getting involved is to visit your nearest National Trust wood, hill, mountain, house, beach, nature reserve or park. If you enjoy what you see, you might think about becoming a Trust member either as an individual, or as a family group or as part of a school group.

Once you join, you have free entry for a year to many of the places owned by the Trusts. The more you are able to explore these places, the better you will understand the meaning of "heritage," and in time, the Trusts hope that you may become involved in some of their work and activities.

Seeing some action

The Young National Trust Theatre is a group of touring actors and actresses who perform plays of true events in real places. They involve their audiences of school children as much as possible by including them in the plot. This might mean taking a castle by storm; working as a maid in a Victorian kitchen; holding down a man while his tooth is extracted without anaesthetic; or getting a taste of what it was like to work under the strict discipline of a head gardener 100 years ago!

In Scotland, several schools have taken over a house for a day and the children have acted as guides to their astonished parents. The research needed to do this successfully is an enjoyable way of learning about a house and its history.

There are opportunities to get involved outdoors, too, and daily litter sweeps along beaches are necessary and often popular. So too are the many Acorn Camps held each year. These usually last a week and groups of volunteers aged seventeen and upwards help in projects ranging from path repairs, millstream clearing and hedge cutting, to digging trenches and building stone walls. Many volunteers return for another year because the camps are fun and offer a good chance to meet new people and make new friends.

But why bother?

The National Trust and the National Trust for Scotland are both charities that can only do their work if they receive money and support from ordinary people. This book has described just some of the places that are under their care. Every place has something to offer everyone. Each has a story to tell and each will catch different eyes and imaginations at different ages.

We have inherited all of this because three people bothered to form a society in 1895 to save and protect, for ever, places of historic interest or natural beauty.

We owe it to *our* children to pass on to them the treasures that have been so carefully handed down to us; to give them what we already have – a passport to treasure for life.

Top: *Children at a Young National Trust Theatre event taste some history round a table laid for tea.*

Middle left: *Every summer groups of children in Northern Ireland take part in daily litter sweeps along the shores of Strangford Lough. This group collected a crammed car boot load of rubbish in just half a day along a 350-metre stretch of shoreline.*

At the end of the sweep each group has a barbecue as a reward as long as they take their own rubbish away with them. Over the summer about 1,500 children take part in this important litter sweep.

Middle right: *A mobile turnip cutter, restored by students of the Inverurie Academy, is formally handed over to the National Trust for Scotland at Pitmedden House where it will join a collection of early farm implements.*

Bottom left: *Three Acorn Campers work on earth steps at the popular Box Hill in Surrey.*

Bottom right: *This Regency fête at Petworth included fencing duels, fire-eating displays, Punch and Judy shows, bands and clowns. A barbecue awaits the cricket teams who have been playing a friendly match throughout the fête – to 1820 cricket rules!*

The Outdoor Places in Part Three

Where to find them

Directions are given to the nearest kilometre and mile, and include, where relevant, map references based on the 1:50 000 Series of Ordnance Survey maps. After each main entry there is a list of associated places from all over the United Kingdom. Extra details and directions for these are given on the page numbers shown in brackets.

30 *Marks upon the Land* (page 66)

Mow Cop Castle is in *Cheshire*, 8 km (5 miles) S of Congleton. O.S. Map 118: 857573.

Paxton's Tower is in *Dyfed*, 11 km (7 miles) E of Carmarthen, 1.6 km (1 mile) S of Llanarthney.

White Horse Hill is in *Oxfordshire*, 10 km (6 miles) W of Wantage near Uffington, on S side of B4057.

The Hermitage is in *Tayside* 3 km (2 miles) W of Dunkeld off A9.

Other eye-catching landmarks include Wimpole Folly, *Cambridgeshire* (116); Grange Arch, Hardy Monument, *Dorset* (101); Rievaulx Terrace, *North Yorkshire* (120); Wellington Monument, *Somerset* (102); Leith Hill Tower, *Surrey* (106); Penshaw Monument, *Tyne and Wear* (120); King Alfred's Tower, The Pepperbox, *Wiltshire* (105, 106); Bannockburn, *Central* (123); Glenfinnan, *Highland* (123); Culzean, *Strathclyde* (123)

31 *A Nibbled Landscape* (page 68)

The National Trust now owns and protects a quarter of the **Lake District National Park** in *Cumbria*. For details see page 118.

Other special farming landscapes protected by the Trust include Coombe Hill, *Buckinghamshire* (111); Golden Cap, *Dorset* (102); Crowlink, *East Sussex* (106); Charlecote Park, *Warwickshire* (114); Kintail, *Highland* (123).

32 *For Peat's Sake* (page 70)

Wicken Fen is in *Cambridgeshire*, 27 km (17 miles) NE of Cambridge just S of Wicken on B1123.

Other areas managed but not farmed include Studland, *Dorset* (102); Town Copse, *Isle of Wight* (106); Eaves Wood, *Lancashire* (118); Box Hill, *Surrey* (106).

33 *The Man Who Gave Away Mountains* (page 72)

Glen Coe is in *Highland*, 26 km (16 miles) S of Fort William on A82.

Ben Lawers is in *Tayside*, N of Loch Tay, 10 km (6 miles) E of Killin and 32 km (20 miles) W of Aberfeldy on A827.

34 *A Day in the Life of a Warden* (page 74)

The Carneddau is in *Gwynedd*, 13 km (8 miles) SE of Bangor, near Capel Curig. O.S. Map 115: 6760.

Nature reserves with information points and/or signposted paths include Longshaw, *Derbyshire* (114);

Ashridge, *Hertfordshire* (111); Calf of Man, *Isle of Man* (118); Eaves Wood, *Lancashire* (118); Ebbor Gorge, *Somerset* (102); Hawksmoor, *Staffordshire* (114); Rhossili Down, *West Glamorgan* (109); Torridon, *Highland* (123); Killiecrankie, *Tayside* (123); Murlough, *Co. Down* (126).

35 *A Mystery to Unearth* (page 76)

Avebury is in *Wiltshire* 10 km (6 miles) W of Marlborough at junction of A361 and B4003. It is looked after by the Department of the Environment.

Other pre-historic sites include Lanyon Quoit, *Cornwall* (102); Castlerigg, *Cumbria* (118); Hembury, *Devon* (102); Croft Ambrey, *Hereford and Worcester* (109); Coldrum Long Barrow, *Kent* (106); Cissbury Ring, *West Sussex* (106).

36 *The Wey Ahead* (page 78)

The River Wey is in *Surrey* and good viewpoints include Tilthams Bridge, Peasmarsh, and Pyrford Lock, not far from Wisley. Boat hire information from Guildford Boat House, Millbrook.

Other waterways or boats restored by the Trust include Shamrock, *Cornwall* (102); Gondola, *Cumbria* (118).

37 *Save Our Coast!* (page 80)

Bedruthan is in *Cornwall*, 10 km (6 miles) SW of Padstow.

Ballintoy is in *Co. Antrim*, 8 km (5 miles) W of Ballycastle.

Good beaches with sand and/or rock pools include Gannel, Pendower, Sandymouth, *Cornwall* (102); Studland, *Dorset* (102); Birling Gap, *East Sussex* (106); Abersoch, Porth Ysgo, *Gwynedd* (109); Formby Dunes, *Merseyside* (118); Brancaster, *Norfolk* (116); Embleton Links, St Aidan's Dunes, *Northumberland* (120); Dunwich Heath, *Suffolk* (116); Culzean, *Strathclyde* (123); Cushendun, Portstewart Strand, *Co. Antrim* (126); Knockinelder, *Co. Down* (126).

38 *On the Wing* (page 82)

The Farnes off the *Northumberland* coast, can be reached by boat from Seahouses (on B1340).

Other bird sanctuaries include Boarstall Duck Decoy, *Buckinghamshire* (111); Brownsea Island, *Dorset* (102); Blakeney, Scolt Head, *Norfolk* (116); Clumber Park, *Nottinghamshire* (114); Rough Island, Threave, *Dumfries and Galloway* (124); Bar Mouth, Co. Londonderry, (126); Strangford Lough, *Co. Down* (126).

39 *Look Again* (page 84)

Dolaucothi is in *Dyfed* at Pumpsaint (A482) between Llanwrda and Pumpsaint. Keep to the marked paths.
Watlington Hill is in *Oxfordshire*, 1.6 km (1 mile) SE of Watlington town, just off B480.
The Pineapple is in *Central* 11 km (7 miles) E of Stirling, off A905, then B9124.
Castle Ward and its tower is in *Co. Down*, 11 km (7 miles) NE of Downpatrick.
Other really good "stop and look" sites include Ivinghoe Beacon, *Buckinghamshire* (111); Helsby Hill, *Cheshire* (114); Hell's Mouth, *Cornwall* (102); Aira Force, Bowder Stone, *Cumbria* (118); Alport Height, Lantern Pike, *Derbyshire* (114); Lydford Gorge, Watersmeet, *Devon* (102); Ditchling Beacon, *East Sussex* (106); Rayleigh Mount, *Essex* (116); Henrhyd Falls, *Powys* (109); Lower Brockhampton, The Weir, *Hereford and Worcester* (109); Toys Hill, *Kent* (106); "Roman" Bath, *London* (111); Ross Castle, *Northumberland* (120); Brimham Rocks, *North Yorkshire* (120); Buscot Weir, *Oxfordshire* (111); Kinver Edge, *Staffordshire* (114); Grey Mare's Tail, *Dumfries and Galloway* (124); Downhill, *Co. Londonderry* (126); Lisnabreeny, *Co. Down* (126).

40 *In the Mind's Eye* (page 86)

Nymans Garden is in *West Sussex* at Handcross off A23.
Mount Stewart is in *Co. Down*, 8 km (5 miles) E of Belfast.
Other gardens with interesting features include Ascott, *Buckinghamshire* (111); Glendurgan, *Cornwall* (102); Knightshayes, *Devon* (102); Westbury Court, *Gloucestershire* (110); Bodnant, *Gwynedd* (109); Greys Court, *Oxfordshire* (111); Powis Castle, *Powys* (109); Claremont, *Surrey* (106); Packwood House, *Warwickshire* (114); Stourhead, *Wiltshire* (106); Threave, *Dumfries and Galloway* (124); Falkland Palace, *Fife* (124); Crathes, *Grampian* (124).

41 *Stone Cold* (page 88)

Riley Graves are in *Derbyshire*, 0.8 km (½ mile) E of the village of Eyam. O.S. Map 110: 229765.
The Cat Monument is in *Staffordshire* at Shugborough, 9 km (5½ miles) SE of Stafford on A513.
Major Labellière's grave is in *Surrey* on Box Hill, 4 km (2½ miles) S of Leatherhead, just N of Dorking.
The Culloden Memorial Cairn is in *Highland*, 8 km (5 miles) E of Inverness on B9006.
Other stone cold graves or memorials are at Maggoty's Wood, *Cheshire* (114); Kingston Lacy, *Dorset* (102); Chartwell, *Kent* (106); Cawston, *Norfolk* (116).

42 *Common Ground* (page 90)

Witley Common is in *Surrey*, near Milford between A3 and A286.
Other commons or interesting woods include the Tree Cathedral, *Bedfordshire* (111); Maidenhead Thicket,

Berkshire (111); Cubert Common, *Cornwall* (102); Claife, *Cumbria* (118); Nap Wood, *East Sussex* (106); Blakes Wood, Hatfield Forest, *Essex* (116); Cragside, *Northumberland* (120); Horner Woods, *Somerset* (102); Drum, *Grampian* (124); The Hermitage, *Tayside* (124).

43 *Planning for Leisure* (page 92)

Great Langdale is in *Cumbria*, 11 km (7 miles) W of Ambleside. O.S. Map 89: 2906.
Lundy Island is off the coast of *Devon* in the Bristol Channel, 19 km (11 miles) N of Hartland Point. It is run by the Landmark Trust and details about staying on Lundy or at other Landmark holiday places can be obtained from the Landmark Trust, Maidenhead, Berkshire.
Murlough Nature Reserve is in *Co. Down*, near Dundrum, 45 km (28 miles) S of Belfast.
Other examples of planning can be found at Fell Foot Park, *Cumbria* (118); Hardwick, *Derbyshire* (114); Golden Cap, *Dorset* (102); Medlock Vale, *Greater Manchester* (118); Beningbrough Hall, *North Yorkshire* (120); Clumber Park, *Nottinghamshire* (114); Brodick, Culzean, *Strathclyde* (124); Minnowburn Beeches, *Co. Down* (126).

44 *Getting Involved* (page 94)

For more information see addresses on page 128.

Links across the Country

Gazetteer

The maps and directions in this section are to help you identify and find other places that are linked to the themes in the book. The United Kingdom has been divided into 10 areas and the places within them are listed alphabetically under each theme. Each entry is considered to be of particular interest for family groups and children, but it is by no means a complete list of all the Trusts' properties.

Most places are open from April until the end of September, but specific times and entry charges can be obtained from the Regional Offices listed at the end of each area or in the yearly edition of the National Trust's *Properties Open* booklet and the National Trust for Scotland's current Year Book. Most outdoor sites listed in Part Three for each area are free to all visitors. All map references are based on the 1:50 000 Series of Ordnance Survey maps. Distances are given to the nearest kilometre and mile. The titles above each entry correspond to the themes listed on pages 32–3, 64–5 and 96–7.

South-West England

See map on pages 100–1

Homes with unusual collections

Arlington Court, Devon, has model ships in the house and many horse-drawn carriages in the stables. Look out for the child carriages and the dog carts too! 11 km (7 miles) NE of Barnstaple, on E side of A39.

Buckland Abbey, Devon, once the home of Sir Francis Drake, contains model boats as well as relics which belonged to Drake. 10 km (6 miles) S of Tavistock, 18 km (11 miles) N of Plymouth via A386.

Overbecks, Devon, has a museum full of treasure that ranges from shells, sharks' teeth, dolls, and butterflies to stuffed birds, model boats and even a crocodile skull! 2 km (1½ miles) SW of Salcombe. O.S. Map 202: 728374.

Trerice, Cornwall, has a most unusual collection of lawnmowers, including some once pulled by horses. 5 km (3 miles) SE of Newquay via A392 and A3058.

Defence towers or mock castles

Castle Drogo, Devon, is the last "castle" to be built in Britain (1910–30). It was designed by Sir Edwin Lutyens (see page 10) and stands on top of a dramatic outcrop 270 metres (885 feet) above the wooded gorge of the River Teign. At Drewsteignton, 6 km (4 miles) NE of Chagford, 10 km (6 miles) S of A30. O.S. Map 191: 721900.

Corfe Castle, Dorset, still has its strong tower but the rest of the castle was ransacked after being captured in 1646, due to treachery. 8 km (5 miles) NW of Swanage and 6 km (4 miles) SE of Wareham on A351.

Castles converted into homes

Compton Castle, Devon, was restored and made a family home by Commander and Mrs Gilbert between 1931 and 1956. The castle is really a fortified manor house and was originally built in 1340 and adapted in 1450 and 1520. Look out for the clever "squint" in the entrance. 6 km (4 miles) W of Torquay, near Marldon.

Dunster Castle, Somerset, still has a gateway which dates from the 13th century but much of the home that can be seen today was cleverly designed and built in the late 19th century. 5 km (3 miles) SE of Minehead, S of A39.

St Michael's Mount, Cornwall, started as a chapel in 1047; then became a priory and in 1425 was turned into a fortress which it remained for 200 years. In the mid-17th century it was bought by the St Aubyn family and converted into a home which it has remained to this day. 0.8 km (½ mile) S of Marazion to the E of Penzance. Access by causeway on foot, or by boat at high tide.

Homes with interesting outside walls

Montacute, Somerset, is a magnificent Elizabethan mansion probably designed by William Arnold who was a brilliant stonemason and sculptor by trade, which is shown by the fabulous details on the outside walls. 6 km (4 miles) W of Yeovil, on N side of A3088.

Massive restoration projects

Kingston Lacy, Dorset, was left to the Trust in 1981 in

the will of Mr H.J.R. Bankes whose family had owned the house and estate for 300 years. The superb house, which contains priceless treasures, will need massive repairs before it can be opened to the public in perhaps 1985. 5 km (3 miles) NW of Wimborne on W side of B3082.

Homes without electric light
Cotehele, Cornwall, still has no electric lighting. See "Serious conservation pressure points" (this page).

Homes with their own generating plant
Castle Drogo, Devon, had its own turbines which ran on water power from the River Teign. There is a splendid switch room between the pantry and the kitchen which is worth seeing, and ask about the amazing candlesticks on the dining-room table! See "Defence towers or mock castles" (page 98).

Good escape stories or secret rooms
Overbecks, Devon, has a secret children's room under the stairs full of dolls and toys from all over the world. See "Homes with unusual collections" (page 98).

Homes associated with famous people
Compton Castle, Devon, was the home of Sir Humphrey Gilbert who colonised Newfoundland and who was Sir Walter Ralegh's half-brother. Ask about the frigate *Squirrel* and the tragic end to Gilbert's life. See "Castles converted into homes" (page 98).
Buckland Abbey, Devon, was the home of Sir Francis Drake after he returned from his voyage around the world in 1580 and from where he planned his tactics for dealing with the Spanish Armada. See "Homes with unusual collections" (page 98).

Homes associated with famous writers
Coleridge Cottage, Somerset, has one room, the only parlour, open to visitors, but the cottage is important because it was where Coleridge wrote "The Rime of the Ancient Mariner". At the W end of Nether Stowey, on S side of A39, 13 km (8 miles) W of Bridgwater.
Hardy's Cottage, Dorset, was the birthplace of Thomas Hardy in 1840. A pleasant woodland walk leads to a small thatched cottage where Hardy wrote *Under the Greenwood Tree* and *Far from the Madding Crowd*. 5 km (3 miles) NE of Dorchester, 0.8 km (½ mile) S of A35.

Places and artists
Saltram, Devon, was close to the home of Sir Joshua Reynolds who visited the house a great deal in the 18th century. There are no less than 14 portraits by this famous artist on its walls. 6 km (3½ miles) E of Plymouth city centre, between A38 and A379.

Serious conservation pressure points
Cotehele, Cornwall, is featured on pages 29 and 33.

Saltram, Devon, has, among many of its lavish treasures, red silk velvet on its walls which has faded over the years. The material behind the pictures is, however, a deep red because the sunlight has not affected it. See "Places and artists" (above).

Odd Discoveries
Knightshayes Court, Devon, is featured on pages 30 and 33.

Farm buildings or collections
Buckland Abbey, Devon, has a huge tithe barn, built in 1300. The magnificent timber roof is held together with wooden pegs. See "Homes with unusual collections" (page 98).
West Pennard Court Barn, Somerset, is a large 15th-century barn with five bays. 5 km (3 miles) E of Glastonbury.

Interesting kitchens
Barrington Court, Somerset, has a Tudor kitchen in the whole south-west wing of the house. 5 km (3 miles) NE of Ilminster at E end of Barrington.
Castle Drogo, Devon, has a pantry, scullery and larder as well as a cleverly designed kitchen. Look for the huge pestle and mortar. See "Defence towers or mock castles" (page 98).
Cotehele, Cornwall, is well equipped. Ask about the racked dogs, the chimney crane, the sand glass and wooden "hutch". See page 33 for directions.
Lanhydrock, Cornwall, has one of the best Victorian kitchens in the country. The large fully equipped kitchen also has a scullery, dairy, dairy scullery, game larder, fish larder, meat larder and bake house to whet your appetite! 4 km (2½ miles) S of Bodmin on the B3268 Lostwithiel road.
Saltram, Devon, has an excellent kitchen which was newly built in 1779 after the old kitchen had been burnt down. See "Places and artists" (this page).

Old shops or displays
The Old Post Office at Tintagel, Cornwall, is featured on pages 39 and 64.

Windmills or wind devices
High Ham, Somerset, is a thatched windmill which was built in 1820 and which was in regular use until 1910. Open by appointment only. Tel: Langport (0458) 250818. 5 km (3 miles) N of Langport to the E of High Ham.
Lundy, Devon, now has an aerogenerator which the Landmark Trust hope will cut the fuel bills on the island by a third. See pages 93 and 97.

Water-powered mills
Cotehele, Cornwall, has a corn mill which has been fully restored to working condition. See "Serious conservation pressure points" (this page).

Dunster Castle, Somerset, has an old mill which was restored to full working order in 1969. See "Castles converted into homes" (page 98).

Villages (or parts) restored by the Trust

Boscastle, Cornwall, had an outer jetty to the harbour which was blown up by a drifting mine in 1941. The pretty harbour was given to the Trust in 1955 who were able to restore the damaged jetty in 1962. 6 km (3½ miles) NE of Tintagel, on the B3263 Bude road.

Villages (or parts) preserved by the Trust

Bohetherick, Cornwall, is a little village above Cotehele Quay (see "Waterways or boats" page 102) and has several houses which are good examples of local building styles and techniques. See page 33 for directions to Cotehele.

Bohortha, Cornwall, is a little hamlet that has been preserved by buying surrounding land and from land given in two bequests. S coast – 1.6 km (1 mile) SE of St Mawes *by ferry*; 4 km (2½ miles) E of Falmouth *by steamer*; or 16 km (10 miles) SW of Tregony *by road*!

Branscombe, Devon, includes two farmhouses, a group of thatched cottages, a forge and a bakery which still produces bread from ovens fired by faggots. On S coast W of Seaton.

Cornish engines

The East Pool and Agar Mine, Cornwall, is featured on pages 53–4 and 65.

Wheal Betsy, Devon, is now a roofless engine house and stack of an abandoned lead mine. 8 km (5 miles) N of Tavistock just E of A386.

Wheal Coates, Cornwall, forms the ruins of the now disused tin and copper mines. Near Chapel Porth on N coast, 2 km (1½ miles) SW of St Agnes.

Wheal Prosper, Cornwall, is perhaps the most dramatic site of all the engine houses as it is perched on Rinsey Cliff. Well worth seeing. S coast, SW of Ashton.

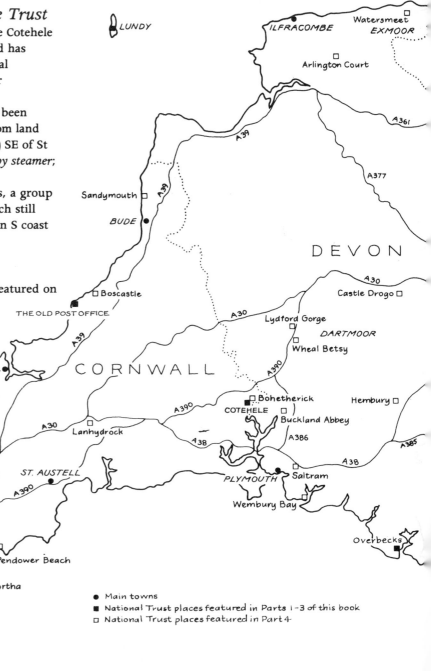

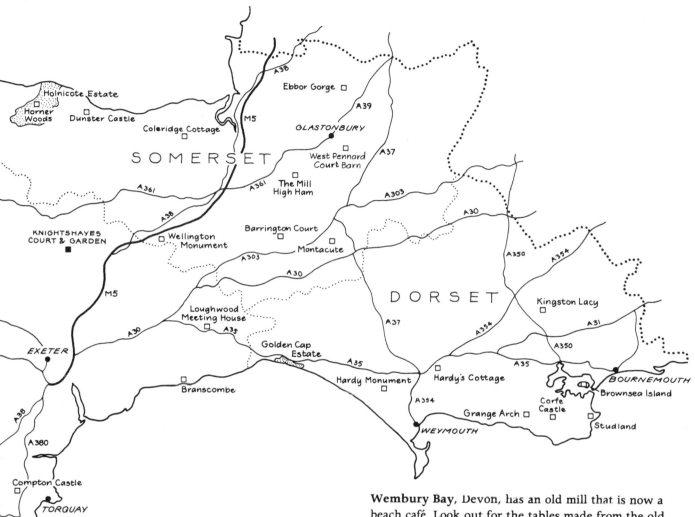

Places of worship

Loughwood Meeting House, Devon, is a remote, very simple, Baptist Chapel built in the 1650s, and saved by a local appeal and superb restoration project in 1969. It is still in use today. 1.6 km (1 mile) S of the village of Dalwood, N of A35.

Old buildings with new uses

Bedruthan, Cornwall, has some old mine buildings which are now used as a shop and café. See page 102 for directions.

Wembury Bay, Devon, has an old mill that is now a beach café. Look out for the tables made from the old mill stones. S coast, 10 km (6 miles) E of Plymouth.
Stonebarrow Hill, Dorset, used to have a Ministry of Defence radar station on its summit, but local funds enabled the Trust to buy the old building and convert it into an information point and as accommodation for working parties. Part of the Golden Cap estate between Charmouth and Eypemouth. Access by car from A35 at Charmouth. O.S. Map 193: 385935.

Eye-catching landmarks

Grange Arch, Dorset, was built as an eye-catcher by Denis Bond early in the 18th century. It has a small battlement with four little pyramids and stands as a silhouette against the sky to the south of Creech Grange, Bond's home. 5 km (3 miles) W of Corfe Castle.
Hardy Monument, Dorset, was erected in 1846 in memory of the flag-captain of *Victory* at the Battle of Trafalgar (1805). 10 km (6 miles) SW of Dorchester.

Wellington Monument, Somerset, is 53 metres (175 feet) high and was built in 1817–18 in glory of the exploits of the Duke of Wellington. There are staggering views from the top. 3 km (2 miles) S of Wellington.

Special farming landscapes

The Golden Cap Estate, Dorset, employs traditional methods of farming to preserve the rich variety of wild plants, insects and animals on this glorious, uncrowded coastline. E of Charmouth, between A35 and the sea.

Land managed but not farmed

Studland Heath, Dorset, is a nature reserve of international importance and it needs to be carefully managed if it is to survive. See "Excellent beaches" (this page).

Nature reserves with information points

Ebbor Gorge, Somerset, has caves and rock shelters in a wooded limestone gorge. 5 km (3 miles) NW of Wells.

Good pre-historic sites

Hembury Castle, Devon, is an Iron Age hill fort on top of a 150-metre (490-foot) hill on the west side of the Dart Valley. 3 km (2 miles) N of Buckfastleigh near A38.
Lanyon Quoit, Cornwall, consists of a huge granite capstone laid on three upright stones. It is all that remains of a burial chamber dating from 2000–1600 BC. 6 km (4 miles) NW of Penzance via B3312.

Waterways or boats

Shamrock, Cornwall, is the last of the Tamar sailing barges. Now fully restored, it lies alongside the Quay at Cotehele and occasionally ventures out on the Tamar. See page 33 for directions.

Excellent beaches

Bedruthan, Cornwall, is featured on pages 80–1 and 102.
The Gannel, Cornwall, provides all you could want from a superb beach. Note how Trust ownership has halted the further spread of hotels and arcades and has safeguarded a beautiful area, rich in wildlife, yet near to the popular holiday resort of Newquay.
Pendower Beach, Cornwall, is a large sandy beach on the south coast, 1.6 km (1 mile) SW of Veryan, 8 km (5 miles) SW of Tregony.
Sandymouth, Cornwall, is another large sandy beach, this time on the north coast, 8 km (5 miles) N of Bude.
Studland, Dorset, has an excellent sandy beach as well as good moorings for sailing boats. N of Swanage on E side of the Isle of Purbeck.

Bird sanctuaries

Brownsea Island, Dorset, is a refuge on the south coast for peacocks, herons, red squirrels and all sorts of wildlife, as well as a large variety of seabirds. There is controlled access to the nature reserve but some parts are left completely for the wildlife, and humans are not allowed. In Poole Harbour near Sandbanks. Boats from Poole Quay and Sandbanks.

Good "stop and look" sites

Hell's Mouth, Cornwall, is where a narrow coastal path along a 76-metre (250-foot) cliff edge converges with the B3301 at a mighty chasm. Vertigo sufferers should remain car-bound while others can brave the exciting path. On the N side of B3301 (N coast) between Portreath and Hayle.
Lydford Gorge, Devon, is a deep ravine of swirling potholes and waterfalls. There is a zig-zag path that is fun in low water and awe-inspiring in flood; and do not miss the Devil's Cauldron, if you dare walk the plank! Halfway between Okehampton and Tavistock, 1.6 km (1 mile) W of A386.
Watersmeet, Devon, provides a gentler walk along the exceptionally beautiful and wooded valley of the East Lyn river. Near Lynmouth on the N coast.

Gardens with interesting features

Glendurgan, Cornwall, has a laurel maze planted in 1833, and look out for the Giant Stride especially designed for children. 0.8 km (½ mile) SW of Mawnan Smith on the road to Helford Passage.
Knightshayes Court, Devon, has a large garden with many shrubs and trees and a most unusual hedge cut as a fox hunt. See page 33 for directions.

Graves and memorials

Kingston Lacy, Dorset, has some unusually large graves in memory of horses. See "Massive restoration projects" (page 99).

Old commons or woods

Cubert Common, Cornwall, is one of the few enclosed commons in England and is still fully grazed by local people, or commoners, today. At Cubert, 6 km (4 miles) W of Newquay, between Holywell Bay and Crantock.
Horner Woods, Somerset, are on the large Holnicote Estate and are an important and rare example of ancient oak "high forest". The best view is from Webber's Post to the SW of Luccombe. O.S. Map 181: 901404.

Planned Leisure Facilities

Lundy Island, Devon, is featured on pages 93 and 97.

Information

Regional Office for Cornwall: Lanhydrock, Bodmin, Cornwall, PL30 4DE. Tel: Bodmin (0208) 4281.
Regional Office for Devon: Killerton House, Broadclyst, Exeter, Devon, EX5 4LE. Tel: Hele (039 288) 691.
Regional Office for Dorset and Somerset: Stourton, Warminster, Wiltshire, BA12 6QD. Tel: Bourton, Dorset (0747) 840224.

Southern England

See map on pages 104-5

Homes with unusual collections

Knole, Kent, has royal furniture from France which was upholstered in cloth of silver and gold in the 1670s. It is an extremely rare set consisting of six stools, two chairs and the King's bed. At the Tonbridge end of Sevenoaks, just E of A225.

Lacock Abbey, Wiltshire, has outside its grounds a 16th-century barn which houses the Fox Talbot Museum of Photography. It shows cameras and early photographs of Lacock taken by its owner, Fox Talbot, who invented the negative photographic process in 1835. The museum is just in front of the entrance gates to the Abbey, on the left. See page 32 for directions.

Defence towers or mock castles

Bodiam Castle, East Sussex, luckily for us, was never attacked and its towers and walls still stand proudly surrounded by a moat. The castle was built in 1386 when gunpowder was in use and in terms of true defence this splendid castle looks stronger than it really is. 5 km (3 miles) S of Hawkhurst, 1.6 km (1 mile) E of A229.

Bramber Castle, West Sussex, still has one part of the huge keep standing defiantly alone. The castle was completed by about 1090 and in its time was one of the strongest and most powerful castles in the south of England. SE of Steyning, in Bramber village, just N of A283.

Scotney Castle Garden, Kent, contains a late 14th-century tower of a castle that has been cleverly changed and added to over the centuries. Today the old moated castle forms part of a large and beautiful garden. 2 km (1½ miles) S of Lamberhurst on E of A21, 13 km (8 miles) SE of Tunbridge Wells.

Homes with interesting outside walls

Hatchlands, Surrey, is an extraordinary sight from the south-west as the west front has three storeys and the south front has two. In fact the house has seven different floor levels all connected by a clever arrangement of staircases. Just E of East Clandon, on N side of the Leatherhead–Guildford road (A246).

Mottisfont Abbey, Hampshire, is a priory church that was converted into a house in the 16th century and later adapted into an elegant country home in the 18th century. The result is an interesting mixture of styles and building methods. 7 km (4½ miles) NW of Romsey, W of the A3057.

Standen, West Sussex, was built in the 1890s and is interesting because of the way the architect, Philip Webb, designed the new house to blend with old farm buildings. He used many different building materials such as local stone and brick and also made use of tile-hanging and weather-boarding techniques. The result is unusual and of the highest quality of workmanship. 3 km (2 miles) SW of East Grinstead on Saint Hill road.

Homes without electric light

Knole, Kent, has very few rooms lit by electricity. See "Homes with unusual collections" (this page).

Homes with their own generating plant

Bateman's, East Sussex, has a 1903 electric turbine alongside an old waterwheel. The turbine was used to charge 50 lead-acid batteries in the house which, when fully charged, could supply enough direct current to light ten 60 watt bulbs for about four hours. 0.8 km (½ mile) S of Burwash off the A265, approached by a lane leading S from W end of village.

Good escape stories or secret rooms

Scotney Castle, Kent, has secret priest holes both inside and outside the castle. There is a good story about Father Blount, a 16th-century Jesuit priest, who survived a ten day search of the house and finally made a dash for freedom by jumping into the ice-cold moat in the dead of night, while an accomplice raised a false alarm about thieves stealing horses from the stables. In the planned confusion, the two men got away. See "Defence towers or mock castles" (this page).

Homes associated with famous people

Chartwell, Kent, was the home of Sir Winston Churchill from 1922 until his death in 1965, and it contains many mementoes and personal belongings, as well as objects associated with World War II. 3 km (2 miles) S of

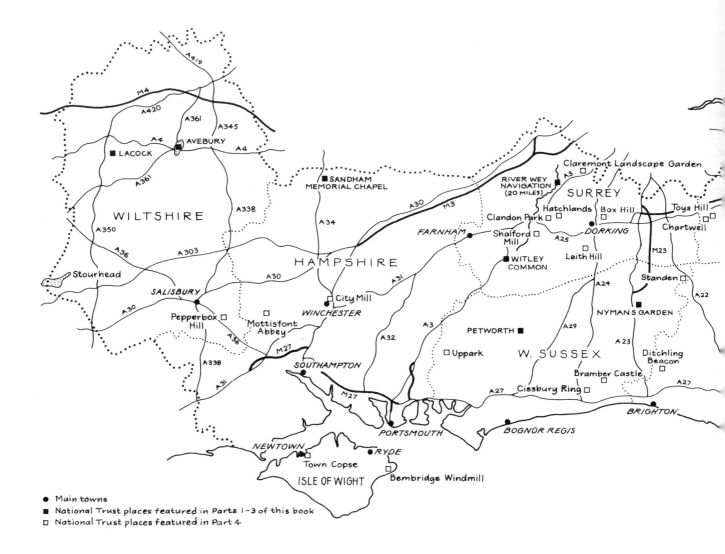

- ● Main towns
- ■ National Trust places featured in Parts 1–3 of this book
- □ National Trust places featured in Part 4

Westerham, forking left off B2026 after 2 km (1½ miles).
O.S. Map 188: 455515.

Homes associated with famous writers

Bateman's, East Sussex, was the home of Rudyard Kipling author of *The Just So Stories* and the *Jungle Books*. He used it as the basis to his stories in *Puck of Pook's Hill*. See "Homes with their own generating plant" (page 103).

Places and artists

Petworth, West Sussex, and J.M.W. Turner are featured on pages 26–7 and 33.
Mottisfont Abbey, Hampshire, contains an amazing room painted by Rex Whistler in 1938–9. The artist painted plaster work which looks moulded and real although it is all on the flat, and included painted

columns, books, a "marble" chimney-piece, pelmets and even a small paint-box, brush and box of matches which look as if they have been left by the forgetful artist! See "Homes with interesting outside walls" (page 103).

Serious conservation pressure points

Knole, Kent, has many fine and delicate furnishings that have to be carefully protected from sunlight (and touching fingers). See "Homes with unusual collections" (page 103).
Uppark, West Sussex, has very delicate wallpapers, curtains and textiles which need to be carefully conserved if they are to last. On the South Downs, 8 km (5 miles) S of Petersfield, 1.6 km (1 mile) S of South Harting; entrance on E side of the South Harting–Emsworth road (B2146).

carrying the sails and the wind shaft. Look out for the Nipper's window at the top of the mill. 0.8 km ($\frac{1}{2}$ mile) S of Bembridge. O.S. Map 196: 639874.

Water-powered mills

Bateman's, East Sussex, has a mill which dates from about 1750 and which has been restored to full working order. There is an interesting display of photographs of the restoration work being carried out by local volunteers. The mill grinds flour for sale. See "Homes with their own generating plant" (page 103).

Shalford Mill, Surrey, is a splendid tucked-away 18th-century mill, part of which is lived in. The mill is not in working order but the machinery can still be seen on application to 45 The Street, Shalford, and the worn ladders and steps tell of a time when the mill saw hard-working days. Children must be accompanied. Younger children will love the dolls' house. 2 km ($1\frac{1}{2}$ miles) S of Guildford, on E side of A281, opposite the Sea Horse Inn.

Villages (or parts) preserved by the Trust

Lacock, Wiltshire, is featured on pages 32–3 and 50.

Chiddingstone, Kent, is a very attractive village with 16th- and 17th-century half-timbered houses. Look out for the Chiding Stone from which the village gets its name. It is behind the houses opposite the church but no-one is sure of its purpose. 6 km (4 miles) E of Edenbridge, 1.6 km (1 mile) S of B2027.

Preserved pubs

Castle Inn at Bodiam, East Sussex, is near the castle entered under "Defence towers or mock castles" (page 103).

Spread Eagle at Stourton, Wiltshire, is near the entrance to the famous gardens mentioned under "Gardens with interesting features" (page 106).

Places of worship

Sandham Memorial Chapel, Hampshire, is featured on pages 57 and 65.

Old buildings with new uses

Winchester City Mill, Hampshire, was built in 1744 and stands at the foot of High Street, beside Soke Bridge. Today it is used as a youth hostel.

Eye-catching landmarks

King Alfred's Tower, Wiltshire, is part of the great garden of Stourhead which was "landscaped" in the 18th century. The high tower was finished in 1772 and celebrated the peace with France. It marks the borders of Wiltshire, Somerset and Dorset. In Stourhead gardens at Stourton off B3092, 5 km (3 miles) NW of Mere which is on A303.

Farm buildings or collections

Lacock, Wiltshire, has a fine 14th-century tithe barn with massive timbers and a beaten earth floor. Look for the doorway that has been bricked in. See page 32 for directions.

Interesting kitchens

Clandon Park, Surrey, has an old kitchen in its basement. At West Clandon 5 km (3 miles) E of Guildford, on N side of A246 and W of A247.

Uppark, West Sussex, has a kitchen which has been restored to look as it did in 1895, with large brick-built charcoal-fired warmers. There is also an older kitchen and a tiled dairy. Ask about the dairymaid and the owner of the house in 1825. See "Serious conservation pressure points" (this page).

Windmills or wind devices

Bembridge Windmill, Isle of Wight, is an 18th-century tower mill with a revolving wooden "cap"

Leith Hill Tower, Surrey, was built by Richard Hull in 1766 so that he and others could enjoy the view from the top of Leith Hill. He was buried beneath the tower which has battlements and which looks like a castle. 1.6 km (1 mile) SW of Coldharbour, and to the NW of A29, W of A24 and S of A25 – easy to get to by car!

Pepperbox Hill, Wiltshire, has a tower built by an eccentric called Eyre in 1606. Some say it was built for ladies so that they could follow a fox hunt; others say he was jealous of his rich neighbour and built himself a tower so that he could look down on the neighbour's land below! It is a good picnic spot. 8 km (5 miles) SE of Salisbury, on N side of A36.

Special farming landscapes

Crowlink, East Sussex, is an area of cliff, down and farmland which is certainly a sheep-nibbled landscape. The steep cliffs fall sheer and are not recommended for sufferers of vertigo. 8 km (5 miles) W of Eastbourne, just S of Friston, which is on A259.

Land managed but not farmed

Box Hill, Surrey, is one of the few places on the North Downs without grazing animals or arable farming and so the plant life grows unchecked apart from the control of the forestry operations. There are many species of wild flowering plants and the whole area is of great interest to naturalists, and well-loved by London day-trippers. See "Graves and memorials" (this page) for directions.

Town Copse, Isle of Wight, has been used as a common source of timber and firewood for centuries and remains as open woodland that is still managed. Just E of Newtown. O.S. Map 196: 429907.

Good pre-historic sites

Avebury, Wiltshire, is featured on pages 76–7 and 96.

Coldrum Long Barrow, Kent, stands by the Pilgrims' Way and may have been the tomb of a local king or chieftain in about 2500 BC. When the mound was excavated in 1910, the bones of at least 22 people were discovered and further examination suggested that they had all belonged to the same family. Some of the remains have been preserved, and can be seen in the porch of Trottiscliffe Church nearby. Between the Pilgrims' Way and the Folkestone road (A20), 1.6 km (1 mile) E of Trottiscliffe.

Cissbury Ring, West Sussex, is a huge Iron Age fort with a ditch and rampart and flint mines that were dug about 2000 BC. Near Worthing, 2 km (1½ miles) E of Findon, off A24.

Waterways or boats

The River Wey Navigation, Surrey, is featured on pages 78–9 and 106.

Excellent beaches

Birling Gap, East Sussex, has a sandy beach and good exploratory pools at low tide. Restoration work is due to be carried out after the area was bought through donations in 1982. 8 km (5 miles) W of Eastbourne.

Good "stop and look" sites

Ditchling Beacon, East Sussex, has superb views of the South Downs, especially at night when the twinkling lights of farms and villages can be seen below the steep escarpment. 10 km (6 miles) N of Brighton.

Toys Hill, Kent, commands one of the finest views of the Weald to be found, and is reached reasonably easily. 4 km (2½ miles) S of Brasted.

Gardens with interesting features

Nymans Garden, East Sussex, is featured on pages 86–7 and 97.

Claremont Landscape Garden, Surrey, is a beautiful 18th-century, landscaped garden with a huge grass amphitheatre, a large lake, a long ha-ha, a grotto, a skittle alley and a bowling green. On S edge of Esher, on E side of A307.

Stourhead, Wiltshire, is a huge garden with temples, follies, grottoes and all sorts of features including Alfred's Tower. See "Eye-catching landmarks" (page 105).

Graves and memorials

Major Labellière's grave at Box Hill, Surrey, is featured on pages 89 and 97.

Chartwell, Kent, has several animal graves in the garden. There are two for Sir Winston Churchill's dogs and one for a dove which was given to Lady Churchill when she visited Bali in 1936. See "Homes associated with famous people" (page 103).

Old commons or woods

Witley Common, Surrey, is featured on pages 90–1 and 97.

Nap Wood, East Sussex, is mainly a fine old oak wood. 6 km (4 miles) S of Tunbridge Wells on A267.

Information

Regional Office for Wiltshire: Stourton, Warminster, Wiltshire, BA12 6QD. Tel: Bourton, Dorset (0747) 840224.

Regional Office for Hampshire, Isle of Wight, Surrey and West Sussex: Polesden Lacey, Dorking, Surrey, RH5 6BD. Tel: Bookham (0372) 53401.

Regional Office for Kent and East Sussex: The Estate Office, Scotney Castle, Lamberhurst, Tunbridge Wells, Kent, TN3 8JN Tel: Lamberhurst (0892) 890651.

Wales and the Welsh Borders

See map on page 108

Homes with unusual collections

Snowshill Manor, Gloucestershire, is featured on pages 4–5 and 32.

Erddig, Clwyd, has a splendid collection of cars and bicycles, including a pennyfarthing ridden by Philip Yorke. See page 32 for directions.

Penrhyn Castle, Gwynedd, contains a collection of slate quarry locomotives and trucks and a fine model railway which once chugged round Mr Wade's garden at Snowshill Manor (see above). 1.6 km (1 mile) E of Bangor between A5 and the coast.

Plas Newydd, Gwynedd, has military relics including many from the Battle of Waterloo in 1815. On the island of Anglesey, 1.6 km (1 mile) SW of Llanfairpwll and A5 on A4080.

Powis Castle, Powys, contains many Indian works of art collected by Clive of India. Be sure to see the sumptuous state bedroom. 1.6 km (1 mile) S of Welshpool on A483.

Roman sites

Chedworth Roman Villa, Gloucestershire, is featured on pages 6–7 and 32.

Dolaucothi mines, Dyfed, are featured on pages 85 and 97.

Segontium, Gwynedd, is a fort which was established in AD 78 and held by the Romans until about 390. The fort is under the guardianship of the Secretary of State for Wales, who also maintains a museum. On the SE outskirts of Caernarvon, on E side of A487.

Defence towers or mock castles

Cilgerran Castle, Dyfed, still has two rounded towers which date from the 13th century. The castle's strong position overlooks the River Teifi. 5 km (3 miles) S of Cardigan, 2 km (1½ miles) E of A478.

Clevedon Court, Avon, has a 12th-century tower as part of the defences of the manor house that was built in about 1320. Additions have been made in every century since then. 2 km (1½ miles) E of Clevedon, on B3130.

Penrhyn Castle, Gwynedd, was built as a mock castle between 1827 and 1837 for the hugely wealthy owner of the Penrhyn slate quarries. See "Homes with unusual collections" (this page).

Skenfrith Castle, Gwent, with a tower dating from the early 1200s, was built as a Norman defence against the Welsh. 10 km (6 miles) NW of Monmouth, 19 km (12 miles) NE of Abergavenny, on N side of B4521 Ross road.

Castles converted into homes

Chirk Castle, Clwyd, is a massive fortress on the Welsh border. It was completed in 1310 and has been added to throughout the centuries. Part of it is lived in by the same family who bought it in 1595. There is a deep dungeon which is as it was in 1300. 0.8 km (½ mile) W of Chirk village off A5.

Croft Castle, Hereford and Worcester, has outer walls and towers which date from the 14th and 15th centuries. But the inside has been adapted into a splendid home with magnificent rooms and decorative ceilings. 8 km (5 miles) NW of Leominster; approach from B4362 turning N at Cock Gate. Signs from Mortimer's Cross.

Powis Castle, Powys, has two massive 13th-century twin towers which guard the entrance to the Inner Bailey. See "Homes with unusual collections" (this page).

Massive restoration projects

Erddig, Clwyd, is featured on pages 14–15 and 32.

Homes associated with famous people

Tŷ Mawr, Gwynedd, was the birthplace of Bishop Morgan and is featured on pages 33 and 57.

Places and artists

Cilgerran Castle, Dyfed, is in such a dramatic position high above the River Teifi that it has attracted many artists for centuries. Among the most famous were Richard Wilson and J.M.W. Turner who is featured on page 26. For directions see "Defence towers or mock castles" (this page).

Plas Newydd, Gwynedd, contains a large mural, or wall painting, by Rex Whistler. It is a painting of the view across the Menai Straits, except that Whistler painted it as a romantic, wild, fantastic view with German- and

Main towns
■ National Trust places featured in Parts 1–3 of this book
□ National Trust places featured in Part 4

Italian-looking buildings and great cliffs spewing huge waterfalls into space! See "Homes with unusual collections" (page 107).

Serious conservation pressure points

Erddig, Clwyd, which is featured on page 14, has, ironically, become so popular that steps have had to be taken to safeguard some of the treasures inside the house. For example the restored state bed (shown on page 14) is now behind a glass screen in a controlled environment so that the delicate fabrics will last for as long as possible for visitors to see.

Odd discoveries

Penrhyn Castle, Gwynedd, revealed stencilled wall decorations in the dining-room during decorating in 1973. When one of the workmen put wet paint on part of the walls, he noticed a pattern in the different light reflections. Work stopped at once and the workmen began to remove layer after layer of old distemper. Eventually they reached the original decorations of the 1830s and that is what you can now see on the dining-room walls. See "Homes with unusual collections" (page 107).

Farm buildings or collections

Ashleworth Tithe Barn, Gloucestershire, is featured on pages 34–5 and 64.

Bredon Tithe Barn, Hereford and Worcester, has been restored after a disastrous fire in 1980. It is a splendid 14th-century barn with a large porch over the east door. 5 km (3 miles) NE of Tewkesbury, just N of B4080. O.S. Map 150: 919369.

Erddig, Clwyd, has an Agricultural Museum at Felin Puleston which houses a collection of local farm machinery used in the late 1800s. See under "Homes with unusual collections" (page 107).

Hawford Dovecote, Hereford and Worcester, is a square 16th-century timber-framed building. E of A449, 1.6 km (1 mile) S of Ombersley.

Middle Littleton Tithe Barn, Hereford and Worcester, is one of the biggest in the country at 43 metres (140 feet) long by 10 metres (32 feet) wide. It possibly dates from about 1270. 5 km (3 miles) NE of Evesham, E of B4085.

Wichenford Dovecote, Hereford and Worcester, is a timber-framed building with a little "lantern" opening at the top for the birds. There are about 580 nesting boxes inside. 9 km (5½ miles) NW of Worcester, to the N of B4204. O.S. Map 150: 788597.

Interesting kitchens
Clevedon Court, Avon, has a buttery as well as a kitchen. See under "Defence towers or mock castles" (page 107).
Erddig, Clwyd, has a bakery and several store rooms next to the kitchen which has WASTE NOT, WANT NOT in large letters on one of the walls. Look out for the fly sticker and the Dutch oven. See "Homes with unusual collections" (page 107).

Old shops or displays
Chipping Campden Market Hall, Gloucestershire, dates from 1627 and was used for the sale of cheese, butter and poultry. It has a cobbled floor and a roof with ten gables. In the village, on B4081.

Industrial sites
Aberdulais Falls, West Glamorgan, are featured on pages 46–7 and 64.
Carding Mill Valley, Shropshire, as the name suggests, used to be associated with the woollen industry. There is an old mill which was later used as a mineral water and ginger beer factory, but this did not prosper and the valley is now a popular beauty spot, although the old buildings can still be seen. 24 km (15 miles) S of Shrewsbury, W of Church Stretton valley and A49.
Dolaucothi mines, Dyfed, see "Good 'stop and look' sites" (this page).

Villages (or parts) restored by the Trust
Blaise Hamlet, Avon, is a group of ten cottages with very different designs which were built in 1809 for pensioners who had worked on the Blaise estate. 6 km (4 miles) N of central Bristol, W of Henbury village, just N of B4057.

Preserved pubs
The Tyn-y-Groes Hotel, Gwynedd, and the Fleece Inn, Hereford and Worcester, are featured on page 54.

Places of worship
Tŷ Mawr, Gwynedd, is featured on pages 57 and 65.

Old buildings with new uses
Stackpole, Dyfed, had several derelict farm buildings that have been restored as holiday cottages and as a joinery for Trust carpenters while others were converted for use as a base camp for young volunteer conservation groups and as an Adventure Camp for schoolchildren. 6 km (4 miles) by road S of Pembroke.

Eye-catching landmarks
Paxton's Tower, Dyfed, is featured on pages 66–7 and 96.

Nature reserves with information points
The Carneddau, Gwynedd, is featured on pages 74–5 and 96.
Rhossili Down, West Glamorgan, is the main feature of West Gower – a beautiful area just 24 km (15 miles) W of Swansea.

Good pre-historic sites
Croft Ambrey, Hereford and Worcester, is a large Iron Age fort which was first occupied in the 4th century BC. It has several defence banks and commands a strong position with views westward to the mountains of Wales. Above Croft Castle; see "Castles converted into homes" (page 107).

Excellent beaches
Abersoch, Gwynedd, has a sandy beach at Tywyn-y-Fach (Sandburrows) on the NE outskirts of the town, 10 km (6 miles) SW of Pwllheli between the Llanbedrog road and the sea.
Porth Ysgo, Gwynedd, is a large sandy beach in a beautiful bay. There are cliffs and a waterfall and stream. On the S coast of the Lleyn between Rhiw and Aberdaron approached through Ysgo farm. O.S. Map 123: 208266.

Good "stop and look" sites
Dolaucothi, Dyfed, is featured on pages 85 and 97.
Henrhyd Falls, Powys, are in a deep wooded ravine, just N of Coelbren Junction, 18 km (11 miles) N of Neath and midway between A4067 and A4109. O.S. Map 160: 850119.
Lower Brockhampton, Hereford and Worcester, is a lovely 14th-century moated manor house with an unusual detached gatehouse. Half the fun is finding the house at the end of a narrow road which winds through open fields and woods. Just 3 km (2 miles) E of Bromyard, off A44.
The Weir, Hereford and Worcester, can be approached by car through a field to a small car park. A path leads to a terraced garden overlooking the River Wye. There are several little criss-crossing paths, steps and bridges and masses of daffodils in spring. Well worth a stop if you are passing on the Hereford–Hay A438 road. 8 km (5 miles) W of Hereford.

Gardens with interesting features
Bodnant, Gwynedd, is one of the finest gardens in the country, with many shrubs and trees and a famous collection of rhododendrons. The wild garden and the Dell will particularly appeal to younger visitors. 13 km (8 miles) S of Llandudno and Colwyn Bay on the A470, entrance by the Eglwysbach road (E of A470). O.S. Maps 115 and 116: 801723.
Powis Castle, Powys, has an interesting terraced "hanging" garden on four levels, packed with

magnificent flowers and shrubs. Look out for the very high yew hedges too. See "Homes with unusual collections" (page 107).

Westbury Court, Gloucestershire, is the oldest formal water garden remaining in England. It has canals and hedges of yew and holly. 14 km (9 miles) SW of Gloucester on the A48 close to the church at Westbury-upon-Severn.

Information

Regional Office for Clwyd, Gwynedd, northern part of Powys: Trinity Square, Llandudno, Gwynedd, LL30 2DE. Tel: Llandudno (0492) 74421.

Regional Office for Gwent, West, Mid and South Glamorgan, Dyfed, southern part of Powys: 22 Alan Road, Llandeilo, Dyfed, SA19 6HU. Tel: Llandeilo (055 882) 3476.

Regional Office for Shropshire: Attingham Park, Shrewsbury, Shropshire, SY4 4TP. Tel: Upton Magna (074 377) 343.

Regional Office for Hereford and Worcester, Gloucester: 34–36 Church Street, Tewkesbury, Gloucestershire, GL20 5SN. Tel: Tewkesbury (0684) 292427.

Regional Office for Avon: Stourton, Warminster, Wiltshire, BA12 6QD. Tel: Bourton, Dorset (0747) 840224.

London, Thames Valley and the Chilterns

See map on page 111

Defence towers or mock castles

Boarstall Tower, Buckinghamshire, is all that remains of a fortified house which once stood on the spot. The 14th-century tower still has some crossloops for bows, and most of its moat. Today it is let as a home but can be viewed from the outside. Near Aylesbury, midway between Bicester and Thame, 3 km (2 miles) W of Brill.

Greys Court, Oxfordshire, still has some of its 14th-century fortifications, including the keep and three towers. The rest of the house was rebuilt and altered over 300 years starting in the 1500s. Do not miss the donkey wheel in the Wheelhouse. 5 km (3 miles) NW of Henley-on-Thames.

Homes associated with famous people

Claydon House, Buckinghamshire, was often visited by Florence Nightingale whose sister lived there in Victorian times. The bedroom she used is on show and there is a small display of things which belonged to Miss Nightingale. Two photographs of "The Lady of the Lamp" show how thin she became during her nursing ordeal abroad. At Middle Claydon, 21 km (13 miles) NW of Aylesbury, 6 km (3½ miles) SW of Winslow.

Farm buildings or collections

Great Coxwell, Oxfordshire, has a 13th-century barn of massive proportions with a really superb roof. Look out, too, for the dovecote over the east door. 3 km (2 miles) SW of Faringdon. O.S. Map 163: 269940.

Willington Dovecote and Stables, Bedfordshire, have spectacular gabled roofs and high walls. The vast dovecote is lined with no less than 1,500 nesting boxes, and the stables were built with living quarters (complete with fireplace) for the grooms. 7 km (4 miles) E of Bedford, N of A603.

Interesting kitchens

Carlyle's House, London, has a "comfortable and serviceable" 19th-century kitchen with a range, cooking "jack" and other furnishings. No. 24 Cheyne Row, Chelsea, London SW1.

Windmills or wind devices

Pitstone Windmill, Buckinghamshire, is featured on pages 42–3 and 64.

Villages (or parts) preserved by the Trust

Coleshill, Oxfordshire, is a farming village with large farmhouses surrounded by dairy herds and wheat fields. Good picnic spot at Bradbury Hill just along the B4019. Village is 5 km (3 miles) SW of Faringdon.

West Wycombe, Buckinghamshire, has 15th-, 16th-, 17th- and 18th-century houses all jostled together. 3 km (2 miles) W of high Wycombe, on A40.

Special skills

Boarstall Duck Decoy, Buckinghamshire, needs the skill of a dog passing in front of special reed screens to arouse the curiosity of ducks which follow the dog to a point of no return. When the decoy was first built in the 18th century it was used to catch the ducks for food – now it is used for numbering and ringing the birds for information! Near Aylesbury, midway between Bicester and Thame.

Old buildings with new uses

Blewcoat School, London, is now used as a Trust store and for receptions. It was built in 1709 at the expense of a local brewer. Look for the statue of a "Bluecoat Schoolboy" over the door. No. 23 Caxton Street, London SW1, near its junction with Buckingham Gate.

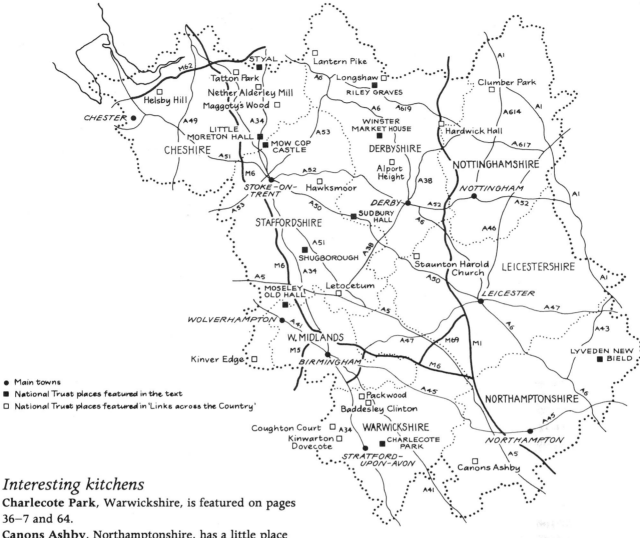

Interesting kitchens

Charlecote Park, Warwickshire, is featured on pages 36–7 and 64.

Canons Ashby, Northamptonshire, has a little place where food was left for passing travellers, rows of bells for different rooms and a speaking pipe for ordering more drinks from the dining-room! See "Massive restoration projects" (page 112).

Hardwick Hall, Derbyshire, contains hundreds of 18th- and 19th-century brass pots and pans and pewter plates as well as a mechanical spit and great fireplace. See "Serious conservation pressure points" (page 112).

Old shops or displays

Winster Market House, Derbyshire, is featured on pages 38–9 and 64.

Shugborough, Staffordshire, has two reconstructed shops in the museum. See "Farm buildings or collections" (page 112).

Old schoolrooms or displays

Sudbury Hall, Derbyshire, is featured on pages 40–1 and 64.

Shugborough, Staffordshire, has a schoolroom as part of the museum displays. See "Farm buildings or collections" (page 112).

Water-powered mills

Nether Alderley Mill, Cheshire, has two wooden waterwheels to drive the machinery. The mill is in full working order after being restored in 1967 and corn is ground from time to time. 2 km (1¼ miles) S of Alderley Edge on W side of A34.

Quarry Bank Mill, Cheshire, provided the power to work the cotton machines featured on pages 48–9 and 64. A waterwheel is being installed again and when it is in position (due 1984) it will be used once again to power the rows of machines in the cotton mill. See page 64 for directions.

Villages (or parts) restored by the Trust

Styal, Cheshire, is featured on pages 49–50 and 64.

Villages (or parts) preserved by the Trust

Hardwick Village, Nottinghamshire, is part of the Clumber Park estate, near Worksop. See "Planned leisure facilities" (page 114).

Places of worship

Clumber Church, Nottinghamshire, is cleverly constructed to seem higher and bigger than it really is. Clumber House suffered two disastrous fires and was finally pulled down in 1938, but the church has survived and it dominates its surroundings today. See ''Planned leisure facilities'' (this page).

Staunton Harold Church, Leicestershire, was built by Sir Robert Shirley in 1653 more as an act of defiance against Cromwell than as a practical place of worship. Sir Robert was arrested and died at the age of 29 in the Tower of London but his church survived. 8 km (5 miles) NE of Ashby-de-la-Zouch, just W of B587.

Eye-catching landmarks

Mow Cop Castle, Cheshire, is featured on pages 67 and 96.

Special farming landscapes

Charlecote Park, Warwickshire, has Jacob sheep and red and fallow deer which control the growth of the grass in the Park, which is as much an ornamental park as a farming area. See page 64 for directions.

Nature reserves with information points

Hawksmoor, Staffordshire, consists of woodland on the slopes of the River Churnet. 2 km (1½ miles) NE of Cheadle, on N side of B5417.

Longshaw, Derbyshire, is just 13 km (8 miles) from the centre of Sheffield. It is a breathtaking area of moor and woodland; 2-6 km (1–3 miles) SE of Hathersage, on S side of A625.

Bird sanctuaries

Clumber Park, Nottinghamshire, is a haven for a large number of birds that can be seen on the lake or in the trees. See ''Planned leisure facilities'' (this page).

Good ''stop and look'' sites

Alport Height, Derbyshire, is a superb spot from where it is possible to see across half of Derbyshire and the width of Staffordshire. Look out for the Alport Stone. 6 km (4 miles) NW of Belper. O.S. Map 119: 305515.

Helsby Hill, Cheshire, for great views over the Mersey and to the Welsh mountains. 0.8 km (½ mile) S of Helsby, just E of A56.

Kinver Edge, Staffordshire, is famous for its extraordinary cave dwellings and rock houses which have been cut out of the soft sandstone. Look for Nanny's Rock and, better still, the Holy Austin Rock. 6 km (4 miles) W of Stourbridge and N of Kidderminster.

Lantern Pike, Derbyshire, has views in every direction. 2 km (1½ miles) NW of Hayfield near A624 and A6015.

Gardens with interesting features

Packwood House, Warwickshire, has a topiary garden of yew trees arranged in such a way as to represent the Sermon on the Mount. Look for the Apostles, the Evangelists and the Master. 1.6 km (1 mile) E of Hockley Heath, off A34.

Graves and memorials

Riley Graves, Derbyshire, and the **Cat Monument**, Staffordshire, are both featured on pages 88 and 97.

Maggoty's Wood, Cheshire, was the last resting place of ''Lord Flame'' alias ''Maggoty'' Johnson, a true eccentric, comedian, wit, dramatist, musician, poet, jester, dancing master – need I go on? Worth a peep, just 0.8 km (½ mile) NW of Gawsworth, E of A536. And bring your dancing shoes!

Planned leisure facilities

Clumber Park, Nottinghamshire, has excellent facilities for caravans, cycle hire and coarse fishing. 4 km (2½ miles) SE of Worksop, via A57 or A614.

Hardwick Park, Derbyshire, has a nature walk and opportunities for canoeing and fishing. See ''Serious conservation pressure points'' (page 112).

Information

Regional Office for Derbyshire, Leicestershire, Northamptonshire, Nottinghamshire and parts of Cheshire and Staffordshire: Clumber Park Stableyard, Worksop, Notts, S80 3BE. Tel: Worksop (0909) 486411.

Regional Office for most of Staffordshire and West Midlands: Attingham Park, Shrewsbury, Shropshire, SY4 4TP. Tel: Upton Magna (074 377) 343.

Regional Office for most of Warwickshire: 34–36 Church Street, Tewkesbury, Gloucestershire, GL20 5SN. Tel: Tewkesbury (0684) 292427.

Eastern Counties

See map on page 116

Homes with unusual collections

Angel Corner, Suffolk, contains a collection of clocks owned by the St Edmundsbury Council. Look out for the "Atmos" clock which runs on changes in temperature. On Angel Hill in Bury St Edmunds.

Defence towers or mock castles

Oxburgh Hall, Norfolk, has a most impressive gatehouse which is a tower 24 metres (80 feet) high. The whole house is surrounded by a moat which gave added protection to the occupants, although Oxburgh would not have survived a full attack. 11 km (7 miles) SW of Swaffham, on S side of the Stoke Ferry road.
Tattershall Castle, Lincolnshire, is a 30-metre (100-foot) high tower built of red brick in about 1440. Its large windows and decorated roof gallery are real giveaway clues of the castle's true intent! It was built more to impress than for strict defence—and it certainly is impressive on the flat Lincolnshire fens. 5 km (3½ miles) SE of Woodhall Spa on S side of A153.

Homes with interesting outside walls

Felbrigg Hall, Norfolk, is featured on pages 13 and 32.

Good escape stories or secret rooms

Oxburgh Hall, Norfolk, has a well concealed trapdoor over a priest's hole near the King's Room. See "Defence towers or mock castles" (this page).

Homes associated with famous people

Woolsthorpe Manor, Lincolnshire, was the birthplace of Sir Isaac Newton and is featured on pages 22–3, 33.

Places and artists

Flatford Mill, Suffolk, provides the setting for some of John Constable's most famous paintings. Willy Lott's cottage is nearby. The mill is let to the Field Studies Council and not open. On N bank of the Stour, 1.6 km (1 mile) S of East Bergholt (B1070). O.S. Map 168: 077332.

Farm buildings or collections

The dovecote at **Felbrigg Hall**, Norfolk, is featured on pages 34 and 64.
The Home Farm, Wimpole, Cambridgeshire, has an excellent museum of farming in a splendid thatched barn. There are also rare breeds of livestock such as White Park, British White and Longhorn cattle and Leicester Longwool sheep kept on the farm, which the Trust hopes to develop. Near New Wimpole, on N side of A603, 13 km (8 miles) SW of Cambridge.

Old shops or displays

Paycocke's, Essex, is featured on pages 38 and 64.
Lavenham Guildhall, Suffolk, is featured on pages 61 and 65.

Windmills or wind devices

Burnham Overy Mill, Norfolk, consists of several mill buildings. Unfortunately the windmill was tail-winded in a storm in 1914 and the watermill nearby was partially destroyed by fire in 1959. Neither mill is open but the unusual group of buildings is worth a visit. 1.6 km (1 mile) N of Burnham Market, on SE side of A149.
Horsey Drainage Windmill, Norfolk, stopped operating in 1943 when it was struck by lightning but it has been restored and although it does not actually work, it is possible to climb to the top of it. But take care. 4 km (2½ miles) NE of Potter Heigham, 17 km (11 miles) N of Yarmouth near B1159.
Wicken Fen, Cambridgeshire, is featured on pages 71 and 96.

Water-powered mills

Bourne Mill, Essex, has a fully operating mill wheel and some machinery inside the mill building, which has been converted into a dwelling. There is a good view of the wheel through a glass panel in the floor. 1.6 km (1 mile) S of the centre of Colchester just E of the Mersea road (B1025).
Lode Mill, Cambridgeshire, is a fully restored and operating mill which grinds corn and sells flour. Well worth a visit but check the opening times on Cambridge (0223) 311894. In the grounds of Anglesey Abbey, in the village of Lode, on N side of B1102, 10 km (6 miles) NE of Cambridge.

Old buildings with new uses

Lavenham Guildhall, Suffolk, is featured on pages 61 and 65.
Houghton Mill, Cambridgeshire, is a 17th-century water mill which is now used as a youth hostel. Midway between Huntingdon and St Ives, just S of A1123.

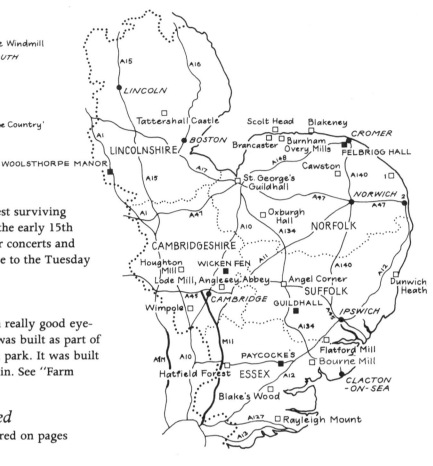

1 Horsey Drainage Windmill
2 *GREAT YARMOUTH*

● Main towns
■ National Trust places featured in the text
□ National Trust places featured in 'Links across the Country'

St George's Hall, Norfolk, is the largest surviving guildhall in England and was built in the early 15th century. Now used as a theatre and for concerts and recitals. On W side of King Street, close to the Tuesday Market Place in King's Lynn.

Eye-catching landmarks

Wimpole Hall, Cambridgeshire, has a really good eye-catching tower in its grounds, which was built as part of the landscape for the whole house and park. It was built in 1768 but looks like a much older ruin. See "Farm buildings or collections" (this page).

Land managed but not farmed

Wicken Fen, Cambridgeshire, is featured on pages 71–2 and 96.

Excellent beaches

Brancaster, Norfolk, is a spectacular beach of sand dunes, marsh and saltings covering 2,150 acres. Access to the sea from the Brancaster beach road on the W and also at Brancaster Staithe and Burnham Deepdale. The beach road is covered at high tide, please note. On the N coast between Hunstanton and Wells.

Dunwich Heath, Suffolk, consists of sandy cliffs and heathland with a mile of beach. Access by a road turning S off the Westleton–Dunwich road 0.8 km (½ mile) before reaching Dunwich. O.S. Map 156: 475683.

Bird sanctuaries

Blakeney Point, Norfolk, is used by nesting colonies of terns, oyster-catchers, ringed plovers, redshanks, shelduck and other species. There are two observation hides. 13 km (8 miles) E of Wells, N of Blakeney and Morston (A149) from all of which it can be reached by boat.

Scolt Head Island, Norfolk, is used mainly by nesting sandwich terns and oyster-catchers. Access by boat from Brancaster Staithe between Hunstanton and Wells.

Good "stop and look" sites

Rayleigh Mount, Essex, was the site of a castle in the 12th century though only the earthworks remain today. Even so it is a magnificent defensive position and worth stopping for. 10 km (6 miles) NW of Southend, by footpath from Rayleigh station, near A129.

Graves and memorials

Cawston Duelling Stone, Norfolk, marks the spot where Sir Henry Hobart of Blickling Hall died of his injuries during a duel in 1698. By the side of the B1149 Norwich–Holt road, close to the old Woodrow Inn. It is not that easy to find so take your time! O.S. Map 133: 153241.

Old commons or woods

Blakes Wood, Essex, is one of the few areas of true woodland which once made up Epping Forest, which covered most of Essex. 8 km (5 miles) E of Chelmsford near A414.

Hatfield Forest, Essex, has fine trees, lots of wildlife and many footpaths. 5 km (3 miles) E of Bishop's Stortford, on S side of A120.

Information

Regional Office for Lincolnshire: Clumber Park Stableyard, Worksop, Nottinghamshire, S80 3BE. Tel: Worksop (0909) 486411.

Regional Office for Cambridgeshire, Essex, Norfolk and Suffolk: Blickling, Norwich, NR11 6NF. Tel: Aylsham (026 373) 3471.

North-West England

See map on page 118

Homes with unusual collections

Dunham Massey, Greater Manchester, contains a really impressive collection of silver including a wine "fountain" and an enormous wine "cistern". 5 km (3 miles) SW of Altrincham off A56.

Defence towers or mock castles

Sizergh Castle, Cumbria, has a strong pele tower, built about 1340 against Scottish border raids. 5 km (3 miles) S of Kendal, close to the A6/A591 interchange.

Homes with interesting outside walls

Rufford Old Hall, Lancashire, is a 15th-century building with additions in 1662 and 1821. The oldest part is the Great Hall with magnificent carvings. Look out for the large movable screen. 8 km (5 miles) N of Ormskirk, at N end of Rufford, on E side of A59.
Speke Hall, Merseyside, is one of the finest half-timbered houses in the country, and it survives between industrial buildings and a runway of Speke airport! On N bank of the Mersey, 13 km (8 miles) SE of the centre of Liverpool, S of A561 on E side of airport.

Homes without electric light

Townend, Cumbria, is featured on pages 16–17 and 32.

Good escape stories or secret rooms

Speke Hall, Merseyside, has several priest holes cleverly hidden in or next to the large chimney stacks. This gave warmth but also meant that it was impossible to locate them by comparing inside room measurements with those of the outside walls, which was a favourite method of searching! See "Homes with interesting outside walls" (this page).

Homes associated with famous writers

Wordsworth House, Cumbria, is featured on pages 24–5 and 33.

Places and artists

Dunham Massey, Greater Manchester, contains four remarkable "bird's eye view" paintings showing the house and park from the air – all done in the head of the artist, John Harris, in 1750. See "Homes with unusual collections" (this page).

Serious conservation pressure points

Hill Top, Cumbria, suffers from too many visitors and there are serious worries whether the house can survive all the thousands of feet that visit it. Famous as the home of Beatrix Potter. See pages 68–9.

Interesting kitchens

Dunham Massey, Greater Manchester, has several large store rooms next to a splendid kitchen. See "Homes with unusual collections" (this page).

Water-powered mills

Dunham Massey, Greater Manchester, has a fully working sawmill. Look for "The Dunham Ripper". See "Homes with unusual collections" (this page).

Preserved pubs

Cross Keys Inn at Cautley, Cumbria, dates from about 1600. It is on the B6258 Kirkby Stephen road, 8 km (5 miles) NE of Sedbergh.
Tower Bank Arms, Near Sawrey, Cumbria, features in *The Tale of Jemima Puddle-Duck* by Beatrix Potter and has a picture from the book as its pub sign. 3 km (2 miles) S of Hawkshead, on B5285.

Places of worship

Keld Chapel, Cumbria, is small, made of rubble and dating from the early 1500s. 1.5 km (1 mile) SW of Shap, close to the River Lowther. O.S. Map 90: 554145.

Old buildings with new uses

Bridge House, Cumbria, is featured on pages 60 and 65.

Special farming landscapes

The National Trust now owns and protects about a quarter of the **Lake District National Park** in Cumbria. The early days of this enormous conservation project are featured on page 68.

Land managed but not farmed

Eaves Wood, Lancashire, contains hazel which is still coppiced, or cut, regularly as a supply of fencing stakes. At Silverdale, 1.5 km (1 mile) NW of Carnforth, just E of Castlebarrow Head. O.S. Map 97: 465758.

- ● Main towns
- ■ National Trust places featured in the text
- □ National Trust places featured in 'Links across the Country'

Nature reserves with information points

Calf of Man, Isle of Man, is an important reserve for Atlantic seals and many species of breeding sea birds. On the SW of the Isle of Man. Leased to the Manx Museum and National Trust, Douglas, Isle of Man.

Eaves Wood, Lancashire, has a 3-km (2-mile) nature trail which ends at Castlebarrow, a rocky outcrop overlooking Morecambe Bay. See "Land managed but not farmed" (page 117).

Good pre-historic sites

Castlerigg Stone Circle, Cumbria, has 38 standing stones in a circle of approximately 30 metres (100 feet) diameter. It may date from between 1520 and 1400 BC but we are not certain. 3 km (2 miles) E of Keswick, just S of the old Penrith road. O.S. Map 89: 290236.

Waterways or boats

Gondola, Cumbria, is a steam yacht which first went into service on Coniston Water in 1859. After working

for 80 years she became a wreck, but the Trust saved and restored her in the late 1970s and she now glides her way round the lake. A trip will not disappoint you. Details from Sealink, Coniston. Tel: Newby Bridge (0448) 31539.

Excellent beaches

Formby Dunes, Merseyside, is a unique stretch of unspoilt coastline between Liverpool and Southport. Most of the 472 acres of dunes and pine woods were bought by public subscription as part of Enterprise Neptune. Midway between Liverpool and Southport.

Good "stop and look" sites

Aira Force, Cumbria, is a 20-metre (65-foot) high waterfall in Gowbarrow Park, 4 km (2½ miles) N of Glenridding, between the Penrith and Dockray roads (A592 and A5091).

Bowder Stone, Cumbria, is a massive rock weighing an estimated 2,000 tonnes, which "balances" on a narrow under ledge. There are steps to the top of this great rock. At Grange Fell in Borrowdale. O.S. Map 89: 258166.

Old commons or woods

Claife, Cumbria, has ancient woods which were planted by Furness Abbey monks centuries ago. Oak, ash, alder and hazel stretch along this W shore of the N half of Windermere and a path leads to the lake shore.

Planned leisure facilities

Great Langdale, Cumbria, is featured on pages 92 and 97.

Fell Foot Park, Cumbria, is on the E shore of the S end of Lake Windermere. In the beautiful grounds there is a touring caravan park, holiday chalets, boat hire, fishing, bathing and picnic areas and a café and information centre. Details from the Manager, Fell Foot Park, Newby Bridge, Ulverston. Tel: Newby Bridge (0448) 273.

Medlock Vale, Greater Manchester, is a little jewel of countryside in the middle of a triangle between the suburbs of Manchester, Oldham and Ashton. No "facilities" except trees, a river and beauty, much appreciated by city dwellers in summer. Bought by money left by Mr J.E. Ludlam. 2 km (1½ miles) NE of Ashton-under-Lyne.

Information

Regional Office for Greater Manchester and Merseyside: Attingham Park, Shrewsbury, Shropshire, SY4 4TP. Tel: Upton Magna (074 377) 343.

Regional Office for Cumbria, Lancashire and Calf of Man: Rothay Holme, Rothay Road, Ambleside, Cumbria, LA22 0EJ. Tel: Ambleside (096 63) 3883.

North-East England

See map on page 120

Homes with unusual collections

Nunnington Hall, North Yorkshire, contains a collection of miniature rooms equipped with beautiful pieces of furniture and fittings. There are about 10,000 items. 7 km (4½ miles) SE of Helmsley, off B1257.

Wallington, Northumberland, has a superb collection of dolls' houses dating from 1835 to 1930. They range from the enormous "Hammond" House which is 2.5 metres (over 8 feet) long to the "Mouse" house which can only be seen through two keyholes and a large mousehole. 19 km (12 miles) W of Morpeth, on B6342.

Roman sites

Hadrian's Wall and Housesteads Fort, Northumberland, show clearly the lengths that the Romans went to defend England. The fort is in good condition and long stretches of the wall are visible. 6 km (4 miles) NE of Haltwhistle just N of B6318.

Defence towers or mock castles

Dunstanburgh Castle, Northumberland, has two ruined towers and a massive gatehouse which stands on a rocky headland. 14 km (9 miles) NE of Alnwick, off B1339.

Castles converted into homes

Lindisfarne Castle, Northumberland, is featured on pages 10–11 and 32.

Homes with interesting outside walls

East Riddlesden Hall, West Yorkshire, was built in about 1648 but has an extension of 1692 which looks very different from the rest of the house. 1.6 km (1 mile) N of Keighley, on S side of A650.

Nostell Priory, West Yorkshire, has a very grand entrance with columns, steps and terraces and a clever extension on the east front. 9 km (6 miles) SE of Wakefield.

Massive restoration projects

Beningbrough Hall, North Yorkshire, was fully restored over a period of three years in the 1970s and a tape/slide show describes the incredible amount of work that went into making the house and stables what they are today. 13 km (8 miles) NW of York. O.S. Map 105: 516586.

Homes with their own generating plant

Cragside, Northumberland, is featured on pages 19–20 and 32.

Homes associated with famous people

George Stephenson's Cottage, Northumberland, was the birthplace of the "Father of the Railways" and you can see the tiny room where he was born. 0.8 km (½ mile) E of Wylam village, 13 km (8 miles) W of Newcastle.

Washington Old Hall, Tyne and Wear, was the home of direct ancestors of the first President of the United States of America, George Washington. In Washington village, in District 4 of Washington New Town, 8 km (5 miles) W of Sunderland.

Farm buildings or collections

East Riddlesden Hall, West Yorkshire, has a splendid barn which contains farming implements. See "Homes with interesting outside walls" (this page).

Interesting kitchens

Cragside, Northumberland, has a fully equipped kitchen including a water-powered spit. See page 32.

Wallington, Northumberland, see "Homes with unusual collections" (this page).

Washington Old Hall, Tyne and Wear, contains an amusing cookery book and a sugar cone specially made in the 17th-century way by Tate and Lyle in 1976. See "Homes associated with famous people" (this page).

Old schoolrooms or displays

Cragside, Northumberland, has a display in part of the old stable block. See page 32.

Wallington, Northumberland, has a schoolroom as part of its Museum. See "Homes with unusual collections" (this page).

Windmills or wind devices

Lindisfarne Castle, Northumberland, has a compass indicator above the fireplace in the entrance hall. The compass is linked to a weather vane on the roof. See page 32.

Industrial sites

Beadnell Lime Kilns, Northumberland, are a large group of pits and buildings of the late 18th century; and watch your step! 0.8 km (½ mile) SE of Beadnell, off B1340.

● Main towns
■ National Trust places featured in Parts 1–3 of this book
□ National Trust places featured in Part 4

Ravenscar Brickyards, North Yorkshire, are an important feature in the scenery of Robin Hood's Bay. Access to brickyards and quarry on foot along safe track of disused Whitby–Scarborough railway. O.S. Map 94: 973015.

Hebden Dale, West Yorkshire, has some cottages and an old mill that are survivals of the wool trade when it was a domestic industry in the 17th and 18th centuries. 1.5 km (1 mile) N of Hebden Bridge, W of A6033.

Villages (or parts) preserved by the Trust

Low Newton-by-the-Sea, Northumberland, is a pretty fishing village, and The Square, twelve cottages and the Ship Inn are in the care of the Trust. On the coast about 14 km (9 miles) NE of Alnwick.

Places of worship

Gibside Chapel, Tyne and Wear, stands alone at the end of a long avenue of trees. Inside, it has a three-decker pulpit which is well worth seeing. 10 km (6 miles) SW of Gateshead via A694, then B6314.

Eye-catching landmarks

Rievaulx Terrace and Temples, North Yorkshire, are spectacular landmarks in a beautiful area not to be missed. 3 km (2 miles) NW of Helmsley on S side of B1257.

Penshaw Monument, Tyne and Wear, is an enormous temple dominating an industrial scene of chimneys, collieries, cement works and smoke. Halfway between Sunderland and Chester-le-Street, E of A183.

Excellent beaches

Embleton Links, Northumberland, are just part of the superb sand and rocky beaches of this part of England, but there are dangerous currents. To the S of Low Newton-by-the-Sea. See ''Villages (or parts) preserved by the Trust'' (this page).

St Aidan's Dunes, Northumberland, is another really good stretch of protected coast. 3 km (2 miles) SE of Bamburgh, E of B1340.

Bird sanctuaries

The Farne Islands, Northumberland, are featured on pages 82–3 and 96.

Good ''stop and look'' sites

Ross Castle, Northumberland, is one of the finest viewpoints in the county with wide views over sea and land. 19 km (12 miles) NW of Alnwick.

Brimham Rocks, North Yorkshire, are giant rock towers that have been eroded by nature into fantastic rock formations. 13 km (8 miles) SW of Ripon, approached from the Pateley Bridge road (B6265); 16 km (10 miles) NW of Harrogate, approached from B6165.

Old commons or woods

Cragside, Northumberland, has 7 *million* trees which were planted by Lord Armstrong. See page 32.

Planned leisure facilities

Beningbrough Hall, North Yorkshire, has an excellent adventure playground. See ''Massive restoration projects'' (page 119).

Information

Regional Office for Northumberland, Durham, Tyne and Wear: Scot's Gap, Morpeth, Northumberland, NE61 4EG. Tel: Scot's Gap (067 074) 691.

Regional Office for Cleveland, North, South and West Yorkshire and North Humberside: 32 Goodramgate, York, YO1 2LG. Tel: York (0904) 29621.

Scotland

See map on page 122

Homes with unusual collections

Barrie's Birthplace, Tayside, is the first home of J.M. Barrie, who wrote *Peter Pan*. Contains several costumes worn by actresses who have played the part. 9 Brechin Road, Kirriemuir, 10 km (6 miles) NW of Forfar.
Drum Castle, Grampian, has a collection of rare moths. For directions see page 32.

Roman sites

Rough Castle, Central, was built about AD 142. It is the best preserved example of a line of forts that stretched along the Antonine Wall, which is also visible. 10 km (6 miles) W of Falkirk by A803, S of Bonnybridge.

Defence towers or mock castles

Craigievar, **Crathes** and **Drum** castles in Grampian are featured on pages 8–9 and 32.
Brodick Castle, Strathclyde, is a 16th-century tower house with extensions made in the 17th and 19th centuries. On the island of Arran, 3 km (2 miles) N from Brodick Pier. One hour's sailing from Ardrossan.
Brodie Castle, Grampian, has a 16th-century tower and a 19th-century extension covered in sand-pink harling to make it look as one. 6 km (4 miles) W of Forres, 10 km (6 miles) E of Nairn off A96.
Castle Fraser, Grampian, was built between 1575 and 1636. You can climb to the top of this castle up narrow stairs that take only five people at a time. 30 km (18 miles) W of Aberdeen, 5 km (3 miles) W of Kemnay.
Kellie Castle's pepper-pot turrets and little windows all add a feeling of strength to this house which began as a tower in 1360 and was finished as a house in 1606. 5 km (3 miles) NW of Pittenweem, off B9171, in Fife.

Massive restoration projects

Culzean Castle (pronounced Cul-ane), Strathclyde, has seen repairs to the roof for over eight years and to the stone work for over ten. There is so much to see and do at Culzean that you will never be bored. 19 km (12 miles) S of Ayr on A719.

Good escape stories or secret rooms

Castle Fraser, Grampian, has a "laird's lug" from which the laird, or lord of the castle, could listen to what was going on in the great hall below! See "Defence towers or mock castles" (this page).
Craigievar and Crathes Castles, Grampian, both have "privy stairs" which the laird used for himself and for visitors he wished to see in private. Ask about the mysterious Green Lady at Crathes. See "Defence towers or mock castles" (this page).

The House of the Binns, Lothian, has an excellent secret passage which the guide will show you. The house also has many stories and legends of ghosts and the Devil himself! 24 km (15 miles) W of Edinburgh off A904.

Homes associated with famous people

The House of the Binns, Lothian, was once the home of General Tam Dalyell who in the 17th century escaped from the Tower of London and fought in Russia before returning to found the Royal Scots Greys. See above.
Souter Johnnie's Cottage, Strathclyde, was once the home and workplace of "Souter" (cobbler) John Davidson whom Robert Burns used as one of his characters in his famous poem called "Tam o' Shanter". In the village of Kirkoswald, 21 km (13 miles) S of Ayr on A77.

Homes associated with famous writers

Bachelors' Club, Strathclyde, was used by Robert Burns as a debating club in the days when he was scraping a living while working on his father's farm. See pages 55 and 65.
Barrie's Birthplace, Tayside, is the first home of J.M. Barrie who wrote *Peter Pan*. See under "Homes with unusual collections" (this page).

Serious conservation pressure points

Craigievar Castle, Grampian, is one of the most photographed and visited castles in Scotland and needs to be treated carefully. See pages 9 and 32.

Odd discoveries

Castle Fraser, Grampian, has an early 19th-century artificial leg in the dining-room. See "Defence towers or mock castles" (page 121).
The Georgian House, Lothian, revealed a cheekily decorated chamber-pot and a portable medicine chest with a huge brass syringe. No. 7 Charlotte Square, Edinburgh.

- ● Main towns
- ■ National Trust for Scotland places featured in the text
- □ National Trust for Scotland places featured in 'Links across the Country'

Haddo House, Grampian, has a poisoned walking-stick! 32 km (20 miles) N of Aberdeen, off B999 and 16 km (10 miles) N of Oldmeldrum.

Farm buildings or collections

Angus Folk Museum, Tayside, is a little treasure house of exhibits, including an agricultural section on ploughing, reaping, fishing, thatching and other rural activities. 19 km (12 miles) N of Dundee, at Glamis.

Boath Doocot, Highland, is a 17th-century dovecote beautifully built for hundreds of birds. 3 km (2 miles) E of Nairn at Auldearn on A96.

Phantassie Doocot, Lothian, has 500 nesting places and a sloping roof, shaped like a horseshoe, which faces south so as to give some protection from the cold northern weather. East Linton, off A1, 9 km (6 miles) W of Dunbar.

Pitmedden, Grampian, has a collection of farm implements and rare breeds including sheep, ponies, cattle and poultry. 22 km (14 miles) N of Aberdeen on A920.

Interesting kitchens

Angus Folk Museum, Tayside, contains a farmhouse kitchen with 18th- to 19th-century utensils. See "Farm buildings or collections" (this page).

Brodick Castle, Strathclyde, has a water-turned roasting-spit, a huge iron range and all the utensils needed for a busy Victorian kitchen. See "Defence towers or mock castles" (page 121).

Brodie Castle, Grampian, has a scullery as well as a fully equipped Victorian kitchen. See "Defence towers or mock castles" (page 121).

Georgian House, Lothian, has blue-painted walls in the kitchen so as to repel flies. See "Odd discoveries" (page 121).

Gladstone's Land, Edinburgh, has crusie lamps, a glowing fire and a bed on the floor for the servant lassie, who toiled in the small kitchen. See pages 39 and 64.

Old shops or displays

Gladstone's Land, Edinburgh, is featured on pages 39 and 64.
Angus Folk Museum, Tayside, has a shop display. See "Farm buildings or collections" (page 122).

Old schoolrooms or displays

Angus Folk Museum, Tayside, has a little schoolroom with inkwells, slates and sturdy desks. See "Farm buildings or collections" (page 122).

Water-powered mills

Preston Mill, Lothian, is in full working condition and the gentle squeaks, groans and rattles of the machinery are a little symphony of their own! East Linton, 38 km (24 miles) E of Edinburgh off A1.

Villages (or parts) restored by the Trust

Culross, Fife, is a delightful lived-in village and many little houses have been bought and restored by the Trust since 1932. The village is featured on pages 60 and 65.
Dunkeld, Tayside, has a magnificent Cathedral but the small streets and houses ensure that Dunkeld is more a town than a city. The Trust has restored and now protects 20 little houses and two shops in this delightful place. 24 km (15 miles) N of Perth off A9.

Villages (or parts) preserved by the Trust

Anstruther, Fife, includes St Ayle's Land, a group of houses and sheds which date from the 16th to the 19th centuries, and which now house the Sea Fisheries Museum set up by local people. 16 km (10 miles) S of St Andrews.
Crail, Fife, has a little harbour and a splendid Customs House which has been converted into a home. 16 km (10 miles) S of St Andrews by A918, on A917.
Pittenweem, Fife, has many houses which have been restored and converted into homes for people today. Some of those near the harbour have windows and gables which look like Dutch houses – ideas brought back by sailors, no doubt. Near Anstruther on A917.
St Monans, Fife, has been a fishing port since the 14th century, but since World War II the fishing has failed and the port has suffered. Many houses were pulled down or converted but the Trust, in partnership with the local people, has preserved part of the village. Between Pittenweem and Elie on A917.

Preserved pubs

Although not strictly a pub, the **Bachelors' Club**, Strathclyde, saw a good deal of alcohol in the days of Robert Burns and his friends. The Club is featured on pages 55 and 65.

Places of worship

Iona is featured on pages 56 and 65.

Falkland Palace, Fife, contains the beautiful Chapel Royal with stained glass windows, Flemish tapestries, carved oak screens and a painted wooden ceiling. 18 km (11 miles) N of Kirkcaldy on the A912.

Old buildings with new uses

Culross, Fife, is featured on pages 60 and 65.

Fair Isle

This unique island is featured on pages 62–3 and 65.

Eye-catching landmarks

The Hermitage, Tayside, is featured on pages 67 and 96.
Bannockburn Heritage Centre, Central, commemorates the famous battle won by King Robert the Bruce and his Scottish Army in 1314. A huge bronze statue dominates the area. 3 km (2 miles) S of Stirling on A80.
Culzean Castle, Strathclyde, has a "ruined" archway in its country park. See "Massive restoration projects" (page 121).
Glenfinnan Monument, Highland, marks the spot where the 1745 Jacobite Rising began. Poised at the head of Loch Shiel, the 20-metre (65-foot) high statue commands a truly superb view not to be missed. You can climb to the top of the monument up a steep and narrow spiral staircase. 30 km (18 miles) W of Fort William on A830.

Special farming landscapes

Kintail, Highland, contains deer forests that are important to Scotland's economy in terms of food supply, exports of venison and local employment. The best access point for information (which is especially important between mid-August and mid-October which is the deer-stalking season) is at the Morvich Visitor Centre which lies off the A87 at the E end of Loch Duich.

The mountains of Percy Unna

Glen Coe, Highland, and **Ben Lawers**, Tayside, are featured on pages 72–3 and 96. "Unna money" also bought Kintail (see above).

Nature reserves with information points

Pass of Killiecrankie, Tayside, has an excellent exhibition covering many aspects of this historic and beautiful pass with its river, gorge and famous Soldier's Leap. Off A9, 5 km (3 miles) N of Pitlochry.
Torridon, Highland, has a single, narrow road with hairpin bends and gradients of 1 in 10 running through this popular mountain area. 14 km (9 miles) SW of Kinlochewe, off A896.

Excellent beaches

Culzean Country Park, Strathclyde, includes a splendid beach on the beautiful Firth of Clyde. See "Massive restoration projects" (page 121).

Bird sanctuaries

Rough Island, Dumfries and Galloway, is an important seabird nesting site. It can be reached on foot at low tide but watch quicksands and incoming tides. Please do *not* visit in the nesting season in May and June. At Rockcliffe, 11 km (7 miles) S of Dalbeattie.

Threave Wildfowl Refuge, Dumfries and Galloway, has observation posts which can be visited within limits from November to March. Geese, swans, wigeon, mallard, heron, little grebe and cormorant can be seen. 3 km (2 miles) SW of Castle Douglas.

Good "stop and look" sites

The Pineapple, Central, is featured on pages 84 and 97.

Grey Mare's Tail, Dumfries and Galloway, is a spectacular 60-metre (195-foot) waterfall, but keep to the paths and watch your step! 14 km (9 miles) NE of Moffat; 32 km (20 miles) SW of Selkirk on A708.

Gardens with interesting features

Crathes Castle, Grampian, has eight distinct gardens contained by giant yew hedges. See page 32.

Falkland Palace, Fife, has a garden that has been cleverly designed to look longer and broader than it really is. See "Places of worship" (page 123).

Threave Garden, Dumfries and Galloway, is the Trust's School of Gardening where students learn about the skills of gardening. The springtime daffodils are an amazing sight. 1.5 km (1 mile) W of Castle Douglas off A75.

Graves and memorials

Culloden Memorial Cairn, Highland, is featured on pages 89 and 97.

Old commons or woods

Drum Castle, Grampian, has some of the oldest trees in Scotland within its grounds. See "Defence towers or mock castles" (page 121).

The Hermitage, Tayside, includes Scotland's tallest tree – a massive Douglas Fir growing at the rate of 61 cm (2 feet) a year and now well over 60 metres (195 feet) high. See page 96 for directions.

Planned leisure facilities

Brodick Castle, Strathclyde, has a huge park in beautiful surroundings. See "Defence towers or mock castles" (page 121).

Culzean Castle, Strathclyde, has a magnificent park with many facilities for all ages. See "Massive restoration projects" (page 121).

Information

The National Trust for Scotland, 5 Charlotte Square, Edinburgh, EH2 4DU. Tel: 031-226 5922.

Northern Ireland

See map on page 125

Homes with unusual collections

Springhill, Co. Londonderry, has a wide-ranging collection of costumes, including children's clothing, in one of the outbuildings. Near Moneymore on B18.

Defence towers or mock castles

Castle Ward, Co. Down, has a tower house which is featured on page 84. For directions see page 32.

Dunseverick Castle, Co. Antrim, just has part of a ruined watch tower and curtain wall of what was once Ireland's strongest fortified place. 5 km (3 miles) E of Giant's Causeway, off B146.

Homes with interesting outside walls

Castle Ward, Co. Down, is featured on pages 13 and 32.

Massive restoration projects

Castle Coole, Co. Fermanagh, was built with Portland stone blocks fastened by iron cramps which, over the years, have rusted and expanded. The *whole* house is being dismantled stone by stone so that slowly but surely, over many years, all the iron cramps can be replaced with stainless steel ties. The house is being restored section by section. SE of Enniskillen, on A4.

Homes without electric light

Springhill, Co. Londonderry, closes when the daylight

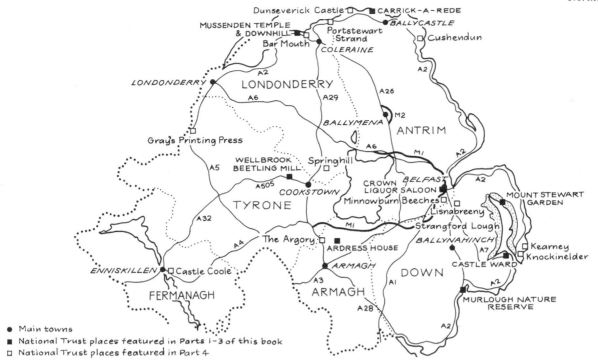

- ● Main towns
- ■ National Trust places featured in Parts 1–3 of this book
- □ National Trust places featured in Part 4

begins to fail. See "Homes with unusual collections" (page 124).

Homes with their own generating plant

The Argory, Co. Armagh, has its own working acetylene gas plant which produces gas for the superb "gasoliers" in the house; and it is all in full working order! 6 km (4 miles) from Moy on the Derrycaw road.

Good escape stories or secret rooms

Castle Ward, Co. Down, has a secret panel which the guides will show you. See page 32 for directions.

Odd discoveries

Springhill, Co. Londonderry, contains wallpapers that were discovered by accident. See "Homes with unusual collections" (page 124).

Farm buildings or collections

Ardress Farmyard, Co. Armagh, is featured on pages 35 and 64.

Interesting kitchens

Castle Ward, Co. Down, has an underground passage that leads to the servants' quarters including the kitchen and a really well-equipped laundry with tubs, mangles, ironing boards and many irons. See page 32.
Springhill, Co. Londonderry, has a kitchen as well as a laundry, brewhouse and slaughterhouse. See "Homes with unusual collections" (page 124).

Old shops or displays

Gray's Printing Press, Co. Tyrone, is where the printer of the American Declaration of Independence is said to

have learned his trade. Today there is an interesting display of old printing presses in a long room behind the shop in the main street of Strabane.

Water-powered mills

Wellbrook Beetling Mill, Co. Tyrone, is featured on pages 44–5 and 64.
Castle Ward, Co. Down, has a water-powered sawmill which is being restored. See page 32 for directions.

Villages (or parts) preserved by the Trust

Cushendun, Co. Antrim, is a little village tucked away in a bay on the beautiful NE coast of Antrim. 37 km (23 miles) NE of Ballymena, on B92.
Kearney, Co. Down, has 13 houses which are protected by the Trust in this attractive village 5 km (3 miles) E of Portaferry.

Preserved pubs

The Crown Liquor Saloon, Belfast, is featured on pages 55 and 65.

Places of worship

Mussenden Temple, Co. Londonderry, is featured on pages 56 and 65.

The fishermen of Carrick-a-rede

The Rope Bridge, Co. Antrim, is featured on pages 58–9 and 65.

Old buildings with new uses

Castle Ward, Co. Down, has a large barn which has been converted into a theatre. See page 32 for directions.

Nature reserves with information points

Murlough Nature Reserve, Co. Down, is featured on pages 93 and 96.

Excellent beaches

Cushendun, Co. Antrim, has a fine beach on which the Trust has been working to prevent erosion. See "Villages (or parts) preserved by the Trust" (page 125).

Knockinelder, Co. Down, is part of a 3-km (2-mile) long beach accessible to the public. 5 km (3 miles) E of Portaferry.

Portstewart Strand, Co. Antrim is 185 acres of dune land including a 5-km (3-mile) stretch of sand just E of Portaferry.

Bird sanctuaries

Bar Mouth, Co. Londonderry, has an observation hide and was bought as a sanctuary after local people raised the money through a special appeal. 11 km (7 miles) NW of Coleraine at the mouth of the River Bann.

Strangford Lough Wildlife Scheme, Co. Down, has seven refuges where wild birds can be seen undisturbed. The scheme covers the *whole* of the foreshore of Strangford Lough which is itself a 32-km (20-mile) sea inlet; to the SE of the city of Belfast.

Good "stop and look" sites

The Castle Ward clock and tower is featured on pages 32 and 97.

Downhill, Co. Londonderry, is the huge ruin of the house of Frederick Hervey, the Bishop of Derry, in the 18th century. A very eerie spot! 1.6 km (1 mile) W of Castlerock, on A2.

Lisnabreeny Glen and Waterfall, Co. Down, is near Newtownbreda just 3 km (2 miles) S of Belfast.

Gardens with interesting features

Mount Stewart Garden, Co. Down, is featured on pages 86 and 97.

Planned leisure facilities

Murlough Nature Reserve, Co. Down, is featured on pages 93 and 97.

Minnowburn Beeches, Co. Down, are part of a beautiful area along the banks of the Lagan and Minnowburn rivers just 6 km (3½ miles) S of central Belfast, at S end of Shaw's Bridge, River Lagan.

Information

Regional Office: Rowallane House, Saintfield, Ballynahinch, Co. Down, BT24 7LH. Tel: Saintfield (0238) 510721.

Index

Entries shown in **bold** are featured in the text as well as in Links Across the Country.

Acknowledgements

This book would not have been possible without the patient help during my research of the National Trust and National Trust for Scotland staff at all the places featured on pages 4 to 97, and I thank them warmly.

I also thank the various advisers and administrative staff at both the Trusts, and in particular John Hodgson, Mrs Marista Leishman and Robin Wright for their help and encouragement at all times.

In addition I am most grateful for help given by Robert Chase of Guildford Boat House Ltd; Ian Horn on Pitstone Windmill; Isador Levy on Cragside; Dr A. A. Mills on Woolsthorpe Manor; Raymond Parsons on the ''Nipper''; Michael Pitts on Avebury; Valerie Rees on Townend; Anne and Barry Sinclair on Fair Isle; staff at the Textile Conservation Centre, Hampton Court Palace; and for useful comments from Alison Crockett, David Holland, Steven Hooper and Edward Pearson. I also thank all the friends and relations who put me up during the research. Finally, a special thanks to my wife Annie – my most ardent critic.

Picture Credits

Professor Roy L. Bishop: 23 right
British Steel Corporation: 47 bottom
Central Electricity Generating Board: 42 bottom
Dick Hillson: 9
A. Irvine: 95 middle left
National Trust: 2 (black and white), 11 (Anthony Kersting), 13 bottom right, 14–15, 26 top, 27 top, 30, 31 top, 35, 45, 46 bottom, 52 right, 57 top, 61 bottom, 66 bottom, 67 top, 68 bottom, 71 bottom right, 76 top left, 81 bottom, 82–3, 88 top, 90 bottom, 95 top
National Trust for Scotland: 39 top, 55 top, 56 bottom, 60 bottom, 72, 73 left, 89 bottom, 95 middle right
B.O. Ratcliffe: 78 bottom left, 79 top right
D.M. Smith Photo Centre, Berwick: 10 bottom left
Tate Gallery: 26
Woodmansterne: 4–5, 25 bottom

All other photographs John M. Parry

Artwork by Madeleine Bradbury, Bernard Fallon, Eric Thomas, Richard Vine

For general information or membership details write to The National Trust, 36 Queen Anne's Gate, London, SW1H 9AS.

For information about Acorn Camps write to the Junior Division, The Old Grape House, Cliveden, Maidenhead, Berkshire, SL5 0HZ.

For information about The National Trust for Scotland write to 5 Charlotte Square, Edinburgh, EH2 4DU.